The Case of Major Fanshawe's Chairs

The Fanshawe five

—Courtesy of Israel Sack, Inc., N.Y.C.

The Case of Major Fanshawe's Chairs

David Loughlin

Universe Books
New York

Published in the United States of America in 1978
by Universe Books
381 Park Avenue South, New York, N.Y. 10016

Library of Congress Catalog Card Number: 78-052196
ISBN 0-87663-317-3

Printed in the United States of America

Contents

List of Illustrations

This Inquiry, I must confess, is a gropeing in the Dark; but although I have not brought it into a clear light; yet I can affirm that I have brought it from an utter darkness to a thin mist, and have gonne further in this Essay than any one before me. These Antiquities are so exceeding old that no Bookes doe reach them, so that there is no Way to retrive them but by comparative antiquitie, which I have writt upon the spott, from the Monuments themselves.

—John Aubrey, *On Stonehenge etc.*, 1663

Plate 15, *The Gentleman & Cabinet-Maker's Director*
by Thomas Chippendale, 1762 edition

1
The Sale

. . . questions are a form of life.
—John Fowles, *The Magus*

IN SUMMER 1973 A BRITISH ex-army officer named R. G. Fanshawe sent into Sotheby's in London a set of five mahogany side chairs. When the chairs reached the auction house on New Bond Street neither their owner nor Jonathan Bourne, who was one of the furniture experts there, at first saw any reason to doubt they were English, and for sale purposes their value was estimated at $8-10,000. That October Sotheby's catalogued them for sale as "A fine set of late George II mahogany chairs."

Even by the standards of Thomas Chippendale and his competitors who kept shops in and around St. Martin's Lane two centuries ago, these looked like superb chairs. They were certainly 18th century and high-style. Their maker turned them out in the ultimate of the French rococo taste, carved from crestrails to feet. The carver shaped the front feet as hairy animal paws. The backs were inspired by the ribbon-back models illustrated in Chippendale's *Director*. My own first thought on seeing a photo of these thrones was that they'd been made for show rather than sitting, but I was only half right. They were made for show *and* sitting. They'd have looked at home in Corsham Court, the great country house where some of the movie *Barry Lyndon* was filmed.

Major Fanshawe had no idea of their true origin. However, he told Sotheby's where he got them. Over in Leixlip, County Kildare, he and his first wife had had an old friend named Nancy Hone Connell. Mrs. Connell had been Irish but not poor. Her passions included horses and she served for a time as Master of the Meath Foxhounds. Her home was called St. Catherine's Park; it stood just outside Leixlip village about 10 miles from Dublin. By letter the Major has described the place as "a very fine small Georgian house," though having lately driven out to look at it I'd describe it as one of the most beautifully kept Georgian estates anywhere. Its driveway turns past stable and gardens, the house ochre under a slate roof. The word "small" as given to period houses by their owners and agents in Ireland seems to mean manageable! The Major recalled that Mrs. Connell had other furniture there as well as the five hairy-paw chairs purchased by her in the early 1920s from the County Westmeath estate of the late Lord Westmeath. However this might have come to pass, Nancy Connell must have cared very much for one or both of the Fanshawes, for when she died in the 1950s she left them St. Catherine's Park with the furniture in it.

Possibly her expectations of their enjoyment would have been disappointed, because within a few years the Fanshawes parted and St. Catherine's Park was sold to its present owner, Sir Cecil Stafford-King-Harmon. The Major retired from Ireland to a lodge near Stow-on-the-Wold, Gloucestershire, where he now lives. But Britons, as we know, have had more to consider lately than their enchanting place names. As his taxes got higher and his living quarters smaller Major Fanshawe felt obliged to sell much of his share of the Connell furniture, including the chairs. As 1973 drew to a close he accepted the auctioneer's appraisal and awaited the January sale.

In London, meanwhile, Jonathan Bourne was having some second thoughts. It has been Sotheby's policy to hire their experts young, and Bourne was then 29. As I've heard several versions of who found what at this point, maybe it will be just as well to stick to the substance of a telephone call I made him in London a couple of months after the eventual sale.

He noticed a structural inconsistency in the seat frames. That is to say, their inside corners looked braced with "pinewood," which was wrong. English chairmakers used oak or other woods for glueblocks, not pine. On this account Bourne first suspected American origin. This modest discovery—even though Bourne's identification of the wood later proved not precise—may have taken more savvy than we'd suppose, since half the original blocks had fallen out and been replaced by scraps that came to hand.

"If the chairs looked American, why did you catalogue them as Georgian?"

"Yes, I wasn't here when they did that. . . . Goodbye!"

Bourne telephoned Ronald A. De Silva, a vice president of Sotheby Parke Bernet in New York. Bourne says De Silva at first thought the chairs might be Irish, but he asked for photographs. The decision to mail photos to SPB New York proved a happy one. About a year passed in getting the chairs themselves to New York, researching them, and showing and circularizing them to major museums and other buyers. When they finally reached the auction block on Madison Avenue on November 16, 1974, they made a new world record price for a set of chairs of $207,500, and it now looks nearly certain that their maker was Benjamin Randolph of Philadelphia. Randolph also made a portable desk for a lodger in his house on Chestnut Street, Thomas Jefferson, and on it (in another house) Jefferson wrote the Declaration of Independence.

The successful bidder at the New York sale was Harold Sack of Israel Sack, Inc.

To the press, auction goers, and most Americana collectors the story might end right here. One more new price record, a coup by the top New York dealer Sack, and a lucky strike for an astonished Englishman. For some reason, however, I usually seem to be arriving when the first nighters are leaving, and a few things about the hairy-paw chairs looked very interesting. Their price, yes. Staggering. The detective work linking them to America's beginning—how good was it? The gap left in their history. Where had they stood for two centuries? Did anyone know, *could* anyone know? Or had they fallen from the sky into one of the stately homes of Ireland?

It's embarrassing but true that the day before the Fanshawe chairs got carried onto the block at SPB New York, I walked around the gallery for half the morning and never looked at them. That day my wife Barbara and I drove down from Connecticut hoping to buy a watercolor or two being auctioned from the Garbisch Collection. There were hundreds of lots—watercolors, prints, needlework, and Pennsylvania Dutch *fraktur* to go through. After lunch we went back and bid $950 for a *fraktur* showing a girl in yellow, a lovely one, lost it by about $2,000 to our alarm then amusement, and drove home. The next week another dealer asked in joke if we'd bid on the chairs—but no, we underestimated them, too!

By the time I decided to go after their story it was January. As things fell out, the delay was probably lucky. By the start of the new year the dust of the market had settled, Sack had resold the chairs, De Silva had left SPB, and the principals felt free to talk about it.

The Sack brothers, Harold, Albert, and Robert, keep shop on the third and fourth floors of an office building at 15 East 57th Street in Manhattan. Besides their salesrooms, the Sack Foundation and Sack

Conservation, Inc., are up there. When it comes to furniture, conservation means a workshop. Over these floors (and those of earlier quarters down the street) since Israel Sack moved his business from Boston years ago, have passed some of the best antiques ever sawed from the log and joined in America. The elder Mr. Sack thought bargains too expensive. "In all my experience," he once wrote, "I have yet to see a successful collection, large or small, accumulated at the bargain counter." From the look of things the morning I got there, his sons carry on in this spirit. In fact, the firm sometimes sounds the lofty note of a Rolls-Royce distributor among the used car lots, as in one of its brochures which points out: "It is precisely the person who says he cannot afford our quality that can least afford to make a mistake."

The chairs had already passed through. (One never made it, but went straight from SPB to the Metropolitan Museum of Art.)

Harold Sack was a compact man, 50 or so, and pleasant in an eye-on-the-ball way. He didn't sound lofty but he sounded careful.

"Ron De Silva called me to come look at a set of chairs. I went up there. Well, they were lined up like a *series* of da Vinci paintings! You have three possibilities—they are genuine English or genuine American or copies. That's it. When it's borderline, throw it over there. . . . These chairs had the mortises exposed through the back legs. Then the back legs themselves. The chairs had the crackled finish you see on American pieces. Well, the English had servants waxing all the time—here the finish decays from lack of waxing. . . . Then there's the waste of wood in American chairs. . . . The hairy-paw foot is very rare. If it's American, it's usually Philadelphia."

How did the back legs mean American?

"I'd rather not explain about the legs. Why go into that? Leave that to the museum guys. Well, I know, every time I get quoted about technical things it comes out wrong. . . ."

(The Fanshawes have round "stump" back legs, said not to be found on fine English chairs of the later 18th century. By "waste of wood" Sack meant the tendency in American and especially Philadelphia chairs to heavier seat rails and other parts.)

"What I saw was the guts of these chairs, and their *complexion*. . . . To us these are living, breathing things! Now their provenance . . ."

From his office sofa he took a call about a cherry linen press. When you're talking a quarter of a million dollars for five antiques, which I don't get to do very often, you're talking provenance, or origin. Here

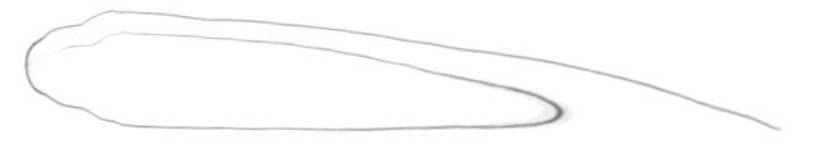

Sack surprised me because he didn't choose to defend Parke Bernet's attribution to Randolph at all. On reflection it's not so surprising, since Sack has always been known in the trade as a dealer who likes an impregnable position.

"We're not dealing in paintings here. We don't need a signature. This isn't a Copley or a Rembrandt. . . . Suppose later it turns out to be wrong about Randolph? If the maker is unknown, if he is anonymous, the chairs are just as valuable. *These are Philadelphia Chippendale chairs—to us living things!*"

He mentioned another detail that put the ball game on the American side of the ocean. When De Silva received the chairs in New York one had a loose splat (the part your back touches). The splat fits in a projection on the seat rail called a shoe or shoe-piece. On the bottom of the shoe he found penciled: *C. Hanlon   John Wannamakers   Phila.*

John Wanamaker & Co. opened at Philadelphia in 1869 selling men's wear, and in 1877 expanded into a department store.

"They had antiques in there," Sack said.

"Who was Hanlon? Is there a connection with Fanshawe?"

"No."

"Is the handwriting 19th century?"

"I don't know, I won't characterize it. . . . Well, we didn't go in there to make a market. I bid these chairs in . . . . It was a sticky wicket because they put them up in three lots—a pair, a second pair, and the single. The first pair went high but under our limit. For the second pair there was much competition, also for the last one. . . . How to play it, you see. . . . We were able to take something from the first pair to buy the others. We were successful. . . . The Metropolitan took one from us, Williamsburg took one, a private collector in Philadelphia bought one, and a collector in Virginia took a pair."

Then they put Sack in front as their agent?

Such an arrangement to withhold bids has sometimes been carried to the point where the participants later bid privately for the lot, in which case it's called a ring. It's also been called unethical. Sack explained he had done no such thing: "It was a complicated deal. We weren't sure we would resell all five. Various museums had limits. Well, I went down to Winterthur* to look at the Du Pont hairy-paw chair there, with the

*The Henry Francis du Pont Winterthur Museum in Delaware. The *th* in Winterthur is pronounced *t*, or you're a square. This variant seems to be more in than right, since the Swiss say the name of their town after which the Du Pont home was named *Vin tėr tör*.

museum gal. Du Pont got his chair from a Philadelphia dealer, I think .... No, not Stockwell." (It was Curran.) "*It* was right. I wanted to see for myself, not from a photograph, that what we had was right. I always listen to what Parke Bernet says and to what the museum guys say, but I don't need them to tell me. ... It was a natural play of forces and I kind of like what happened, that we could go in there. That sometimes even in a recession you can make a new record."

Somebody came in.

"It was a nice thing for Major Fanshawe too," Sack said, smiling.

That afternoon I called on Ronald De Silva at *The Magazine Antiques*.

Having resigned from SPB in the past month, he had just gone on *Antiques*' masthead as advertising sales manager. De Silva has since quit *Antiques* as well and set up as a dealer on Madison Avenue. At 35 he looked tall, quick, and decisive. Some time after college he studied at Winterthur under Charles Montgomery. From there he went to "The largest firm of art auctioneers in the world," where for four years he headed its Americana section, which includes furniture.

Antiques usually sell best on their home turf, and De Silva said that when Jonathan Bourne came to do a tour in the New York branch he had alerted him to watch his London salesrooms later on for stray American items. "I told Johnny when he was over here that an American piece may bring five or ten times in New York what it will in London." (From *Country Life* and other English sources you get the idea there are no American antiques—only Yankee buyers!)

A connection of this kind clicked when the photos from Bourne arrived late in 1973, and if De Silva's recollection of this detail is clear the London catalogue came in the same mail. He remembered a hairy-paw chair in the Blackwell parlor at Winterthur that looked more than a little like Sotheby's pictures. This was a high-powered chair. In 1948 Du Pont bought it from Charles A. Curran in Philadelphia, according to whose background information it descended in the family of Benjamin Randolph's second wife.* The local tradition or rumor had it that Randolph kept this chair with certain others in his ware room to show his patrons, leaving them finally to his widow. Each of these "sample" chairs is different and at least six have survived. All but one are the *ne plus ultra* of the Chippendale rococo style.

*C. F. Hummel letter to author October 7, 1976.

The only thing wrong with the samples is that nobody has ever been able to document them. Randolph's will, signed at Trenton in 1790, mentions no furniture. Winterthur's curator, Charles Hummel, remains unconvinced that his chair was made by Randolph. Neither he nor Sack disputes that the six came down from Mary Fenimore Randolph's son; but on the question of origin in her husband's shop Hummel declines to accept the unproved.*

In any case, as one of the Metropolitan Museum people remarked later, where old furniture is concerned documentary evidence is nearly always mushy. Attributions of art have always been a dime a dozen—this has been called "putting a name on it." Antiques didn't generally start out as heirlooms, and the tradesmen's bills, wills, and inventories identify them with only varying probability. Inventories for probate can be especially vexing. What seems at first a feast of documentation often proves for our purposes like one of those box lunches with nothing really good in it, weighted down by a smelly apple. Once in a great while an artist painted a surviving family piece into a portrait of the period, illuminating it for us like a lightning flash. One chair in a hundred may still carry its maker's name or label, and in just one piece any place did somebody scrawl: "*This desk was maid in the year 1769 buy Benjm Burnam that sarvfed his time in Felledlfey.*" Burnham worked in Colchester, Connecticut. His desk is in the Met's American Wing and this inscription has helped to save him from oblivion.

A printed label glued in a chair, if it's not an old ad trimmed from a newspaper, is usually accepted as a birth certificate. Such a piece not only commands a high price but offers a benchmark on which other attributions to that maker are aligned. In fact this too is slippery ground. One of the rare chairs that carries a Benjamin Randolph label belongs to the M. & M. Karolik Collection in the Boston Museum of Fine Arts. As the Karolik chair has long been up front in the literature as just such a benchmark, I was a little surprised awhile ago to see its back on a period armchair shown in Herbert Cescinky's *English Furniture*. Evidently this pattern, a lovely one, was much copied in Pennsylvania. I wrote a note to the museum's American furniture curator, Jonathan Fairbanks, asking about this, and he replied: "Your letter makes some very interesting points. We now believe that the so-called Randolph chairs at the Museum of Fine Arts are nineteenth

*Charles F. Hummel, *A Winterthur Guide to American Chippendale Furniture* (New York: Crown Publishers, 1976).

century copies—not genuine eighteenth century chairs at all. But one of the chairs does bear a genuine eighteenth century Randolph label. This in no way proves that the chairs were made in the eighteenth century, however." In other words, the Karolik chairs may not even be of the period, which in their situation is an embarrassing thing not to be. Randolph died in 1791. The doubts about the labeled Karolik chair, which lately has been shown and studied at Yale, go to its color and other atypical details, including a trace of stain around the label.

Might SPB (De Silva) now be tying the Fanshawe chairs to another one Randolph never saw—a look-alike at Winterthur of uncertain provenance that actually came to Philadelphia long ago in a sailing ship?

There's a set of carved mahogany side chairs in Arundel Castle, Sussex, dating about 1760 which closely resembles two or three of the samples. An owner of the first sample, Henry W. Erving of Hartford, went to his death convinced his side chair was English, and two leading antiquarians of his day, Lockwood and Nutting, seemed to agree. The American origin of all six samples has since been established on their construction—or Harold Sack would have been in no hurry to look at Du Pont's. The only wing chair of the lot, a hairy-paw, made a then record $33,000 back in 1929 at the sale of the Howard Reifsnyder Collection. It went to the Philadelphia Museum. Three of the others have also found their way into large museums whose study collections are now usually open to investigation by all comers.

Collectors, dealers, and curators are learning to greet such important furniture finds with a curiosity that is more than *pro forma*. Meanwhile a buyer who gets booby-trapped has plenty of select company, and here's one little horror story which may illustrate why the Fanshawes were not at the start besieged by eager takers:

A year or two before Bourne was giving the consignment in London his attention, the Henry Ford Museum in Dearborn, Michigan, happened to purchase a Brewster chair. A Brewster is one of those lathe-turned stickwork jobs that only a Puritan elder knew how to relax in. They are rare. Just two or three 17th-century American examples have been found. This piece passed from a porch in Deer Isle, Maine, through several dealers. Although it was of white oak instead of ash and lacked a couple of spindles, the chair looked authentic enough. After it was traded up twice, a leading New Hampshire dealer, Roger Bacon, sold it for about $9,000 to the Ford Museum. The museum's staff editor then ran its photo on the cover of the collection's *American Furniture* booklet. Bacon also published it in *National Antiques Review*. Then things hit the fan. It came to be heard that a woodcarver in North Scituate, Rhode Island, named Armand La Montagne, was now claiming he had made the chair as a hoax. La Montagne is not only an accomplished wood sculptor but also an ex-member of the Rhode Island State Police. Actually the ancient oak tree from which the chair was turned had been felled by La Montagne himself. Rather than taking any money for his creation, he simply gave it to a friend. The friend planted it on the porch of his house in Deer Isle. He then allowed a dealer from nearby Belfast to discover it, but not until the maker had brushed a gray enamel over the Pilgrim-black undercoat and soaked the chair in Penobscot Bay. From the Belfast dealer the chair passed to one in Brunswick, who sold it, reportedly for something under a thousand dollars, to Roger Bacon.

When the ill tidings reached Bacon he called up the Ford Museum's president and offered to take the chair back for reexamination. He was told the museum had already reexamined it and saw no reason to send it back. As more details reached the curators in Dearborn, they still found themselves loath to believe that Armand La Montagne could have done such a thing. La Montagne then produced the two missing spindles, a piece of stock from which the legs were turned, and the recollection that he had drilled the stretcher and spindle holes with an electric drill rather than an early brace and auger. When the chair was finally x-rayed at Dearborn, this proved to be the case. "Those people think they're infallible, you know," La Montagne was reported in the press to have said. Having earlier been asked to leave the Wadsworth Atheneum in Hartford for commenting too loudly on the shortcomings in the Nutting Collection furniture there, La Montagne thus took his revenge on academe. He has since observed that the Ford Museum "should've been more concerned about the chair's history. If they'd checked they'd have found out that in 1969 it was still a tree."

A spokesman for the museum explained to Sam Pennington, the editor of *Maine Antique Digest*, that at the time of purchase their conservation laboratory wasn't fully equipped, and that in future all proposed accessions will pass through the lab. Also, everything already on board might be carried to the lab as time permits. A spokesperson for the seller (Roger Bacon) told Pennington they had seen nothing amiss with the chair and that once things started moving it was like falling dominoes—nothing could stop it. Nobody seems quite sure just who decided the piece was antique; apparently La Montagne never said it was. Possibly one of the Maine dealers first misspoke himself, but then the French have a saying, "The absent are always wrong."*

Important collectors of Philadelphia furniture have also been left out front when the music stopped. In New Haven a couple of years ago, two Yale seniors catalogued a small show, "Forgeries and Restorations in American Furniture," in which both the mint antiques and the mistakes were supplied by the Garvan Collection. One Chippendale chair was found to be only a crestrail and splat with the rest added, while a Philadelphia walnut chair, long a prize of the collection, stood announced on new claw-and-ball feet and spliced-on back legs, the job having been brushed with dark varnish and then heated to produce crackle. A "Pilgrim" ladderback turned out made as a reproduction about 1920 by Wallace Nutting.

Yet the Maxim Karoliks, the Ford curators, and the Francis P. Garvans—all of whom have come up with many more winners than losers—would have thought twice before writing a big check for a set of "Randolph" chairs found in a stately home of Ireland.

It happened that Sotheby's catalogue was mailed to a dealer in York, Pennsylvania, named Joe Kindig III. Kindig knew as well as De Silva what the Winterthur sample looked like and now he had a picture from London of its apparent mates, miscatalogued as English. He got on the phone to Sotheby's New Bond Street. Bourne and De Silva talked this over. The catalogue had gone all over the world. Also, the chairs consigned to the auction house still belonged to Major Fanshawe. There seemed to be some chance of the auction house's getting shut out if a savvy dealer like Kindig found the owner at Stow-on-the-Wold, got him thinking that things weren't going so smashingly at Sotheby's, and made an offer. Now Sotheby's withdrew the chairs from its January sale and flew them to New York.

Some time after they were unpacked, De Silva saw that one of the mahogany splat shoes had come adrift. He found the *C. Hanlon Wannamakers* line penciled on the shoe's underside.

"That must have made your day?"

*This may seem the place to stick in a little preachment on the dangers of impulse buying, but we were pleased to sell the Henry Ford Museum a tole lighthouse coffee pot just about then, and I can testify that they were slow payers (like four or five months).

"That made my day."

The Roman numeral struck next to the inscription with a chisel (VII) told him the chairs could not form an original set of five but were part of a set once numbering, he supposed, as many as 18 or 24. The Met's chair is marked VII. The Philadelphia collector's is VIII. The pair now owned by Virginia collectors, a man and wife, are VIIII and X, and Colonial Williamsburg's is XIII.* The shoe of chair VIIII is inscribed *C. Hanlon J Wannamaker*. On VII only *Phila* is added. There are no other writings on the Fanshawes or on Winterthur's chair, which is numbered II.

One day a little later on, De Silva and his assistant, Bill Stahl, loaded two of the Fanshawes into a car and headed for Delaware. When they set them down at Winterthur, De Silva knew they had hold of the brass ring. Du Pont's sample was a visual replica.

Were they all joined on the same bench?

In the 18th century furniture mahogany came from Jamaica, Cuba, San Domingo, or Honduras, and merchant ships landed the logs and planks in colonial as well as British ports. English and American cabinetmakers parted, however, on their choices of cheaper materials for parts like drawer interiors, backboards, and bracing. In America these nearly always were made of pine or softwoods such as cedar, chestnut, or poplar. The British favored oak or other hardwoods. It occurred to De Silva that a lab analysis of the secondary woods might now nail down regional origin as well as one provenance for all six chairs.

The two Fanshawes' upholstery was stripped back and thin wedges shaved from the glueblocks in their frames. One of the museum conservators then slid the wedges into a microscope. As with one original block in the second sample, he found them to be of American eastern white cedar, an evergreen that grew in the swamps of New Jersey and Virginia. Benjamin Randolph and some other Philadelphia makers used white cedar for corner blocks.† The primary mahogany matched the sample chair's, and so did tool marks left in the wood about 200 years before. Winterthur's chair had started out with the Fanshawe five.

De Silva said that Nicholas B. Wainwright's book, *Colonial Gran-*

*The present private owners of chairs VIII, VIIII, and X, who've been generous in lending to shows, are leery of being identified in print.

† The labeled Randolph chair in the Garvan Collection at Yale has an original block of white cedar. The label in both this and the suspect Boston Museum chair advertise Randolph to be then *"at the Sign of the Golden Ball in Chestnut Street."*

deur in Philadelphia: The House and Furniture of General John Cadwalader (Historical Society of Pennsylvania, 1964), reproduced two paintings by Charles Willson Peale. The family portrait showed a hairy-paw card table, and the other one the General's younger brother Lambert, painted in 1770. In his portrait Lambert leans on the unmistakable back of one of these chairs. Wainwright, who in 1964 had never heard of the Fanshawes, commented: "The supposition that the chair had recently been purchased by John Cadwalader has appeal. He had the money to buy it, in his hairy-paw card table he owned a piece like it, in 1769 and 1770 he was buying furniture, it was he who commissioned the portrait, and Peale's use of this highly prized chair in the picture may well have been at John Cadwalader's request."

So probably, Wainwright adds of the Du Pont sample chair, "there was at least one other like it."

And now the card table:

Peale took that and posed the General and his family by and on it in 1772.

Back in 1927 Samuel W. Woodhouse, Jr. of the Philadelphia Museum linked the sample chairs to Randolph through his stepson Nathaniel Fenimore: "Five of the six sample chairs have been purchased from the descendants of Nathaniel Fenimore." Of this card table he noted, "the leg of the Cadwalader card table is merely the leg of the second chair elongated. The carving of the skirt of the card table and the skirt of this second chair are virtually identical."*

Something better than old wives' tales had survived, for Peale's brush had put this furniture in one of the great Philadelphia houses.

As the November 1974 auction date approached, all this was enough to bring in the Metropolitan Museum, Colonial Williamsburg, and Sack.

Now a little history:

Around 1770 Philadelphia was the Athens of the New World. Looking through the Wainwright book, I saw why nobody laughed in that city at the name Cadwalader. At 26 John Cadwalader married an heiress. At the time of the wedding in September 1768, his bride Elizabeth Lloyd owned 3,691 acres of land and 78 slaves in Talbot and

*S. W. Woodhouse, Jr., "Benjamin Randolph of Philadelphia," *Antiques*, May 1927. See also Samuel W. Woodhouse, Jr., "More About Benjamin Randolph," *Antiques*, January 1930. Both articles are reprinted in John J. Snyder, Jr. (ed.), *Philadelphia Furniture & Its Makers* (New York: Main Street / Universe Books, 1975), pp. 33–43.

Kent Counties, Maryland, with more in prospect.* The next June, Betsy Cadwalader's father, Colonel Edward Lloyd, a planter of Wye House on Maryland's Eastern Shore, advanced his new son-in-law money to buy the Samuel Rhoads house on Second Street between Spruce and Union, which cost £2,650. Betsy's mother had just died, and besides starting the remodeling of their Philadelphia townhouse, the young couple visited in Maryland and Virginia.

In this connection George Washington's diary entries for August 14 and 15, 1769, written during his stay at Berkeley Springs, a resort in western Virginia, are interesting:

> 14. Colo. Loyd, Mr. Cadwallader and Lady, Mrs. Dalton and Daughter, and Miss Terrett, dind with us.
> 15. Had my Horses brought in to carry Colo. Loyd as far as Hedge's on his return home and rid with him as far as Sleepy Creek. . . .

Fitzpatrick's *Diaries of George Washington* (I, 341) notes of Colo. Loyd: "James Lloyd (?) of Annapolis, Maryland (Toner)." Later on, Washington did dine with a Colonel James Lloyd at Annapolis, but the company in August 1769 suggests his guest may have been Colonel Edward Lloyd of Wye House. In either case, it seems likely that the Lloyds introduced the young Cadwalader to Washington.

By that fall work on the Cadwaladers' Second Street house was well underway. Accounts survive (in the Historical Society of Pennsylvania) showing that some of their finer pieces of furniture came from the shops of Benjamin Randolph and Thomas Affleck. On October 10, 1769, Randolph was credited £94.15 for unspecified furniture. A bill from Affleck a year later for £114.3 lists mahogany pieces he supplied then, but no side chairs are among them. The carving of the parlor woodwork was mainly entrusted to Randolph. There are bills from masons, bricklayers, plasterers, painters, iron mongers, coppersmiths, upholsterers (or "upholders"), and dry goods suppliers. What we don't see, of course, are bills now lost.

After the house was finished, Washington, the Cadwaladers' strapping and genial dinner host at Berkeley Springs, came to dine three times. In 1774 John Adams wrote home: "We visited a Mr. Cadwallader a gentleman of large Fortune, a grand and elegant House and Furniture."

*Some fifty years later, the noted abolitionist, orator, and journalist Frederick Douglas was born in slavery on the Lloyd plantation.

Cadwalader, who was to die at 44, also had what we call machismo. He had an eye for the girls and for bedding them in the grand style. He hunted, fished, played billiards, danced and gambled, and was said to be one of Philadelphia's best ice skaters. (The bulge Peale shows in his waistcoat seems to have been tailored padding.) When it came to revolution, he meant business. Cadwalader didn't cross the Delaware with Washington on Christmas night 1776, but just after dark on that desperate evening at McKonkey's Ferry the Commander-in-Chief sent him a little note: *"Notwithstanding the discouraging Accounts I have received from Col Read of what might be expected from the Operation below, I am determined, as the Night is favourable, to cross the River and make the Attack upon Trenton in the Morning. If you can do nothing real, at least create as great a diversion as possible. I am Sir Yr. most obt. Servt. G Washington."* Two days later Cadwalader succeeded in taking about 1,500 half-frozen militia across the river and was joined by Washington in the night march to escape encirclement and attack Princeton. When Cadwalader was trying to form his line of militiamen in front of Mawhood's brigade, Washington is said to have ridden among them shouting, "Parade with us, my brave fellows—there is but a handfull of the enemy, and we will have them directly!" They were taking musket fire, and his aide covered his face with his hat so as not to see the C-in-C shot off his horse. British General Howe, who wasn't then in New Jersey, later billeted himself for a few days in Cadwalader's Second Street house.

Through the darker days of the war, Washington thought of Cadwalader as his staunch friend and lieutenant: "a military genius, of a decisive and independent spirit, properly impressed with the necessity of order and discipline and of sufficient vigor to enforce it." This sounds like fitness report language by a commander who'd had his fill of dawdlers, malcontents, and nonproducers. Yet Cadwalader's service too turned sporadic. He retired for a time to his Kent County plantation, turning down a commission as brigadier in the Continentals. He seems to have attended rather than commanded troops in the defeats at the Brandywine and Germantown. In the winter of Valley Forge a movement gathered to put Horatio Gates, the victor of Saratoga, at the head of the army. When General Thomas Conway agitated for Washington's removal from command, however, Cadwalader dueled Conway and shot him in the face. He said, "Well, I've stopped his damned lying mouth for a time anyway." Major General Thomas Mifflin, another dissident who quit as quartermaster general, nearly got an invitation, too. "To Washington's expressed amusement, Mifflin had to engage in some fancy footwork to keep from being called out by General Cadwalader."*

In February 1776, before he helped carry the day at Princeton, John Cadwalader's young wife died suddenly. The family said it was partly from dread of his going, but more likely Betsy Cadwalader's death was caused by the birth of their third daughter, Maria. Her coffin was made of red cedar by Affleck. The golden couple's days of splendor in their Second Street house had run to just five years. After campaigning in the snows and mud, Cadwalader was consoled by the baby's nurse, Anne Dingwell. In January 1779, the General remarried; his new wife was Dr. Phineas Bond's daughter. At last in 1786, loaded with honors and a second family, he passed the winter at Shrewsbury plantation, and after some duck hunting on the Sassafras River came down with pneumonia and died. Many years later John Cadwalader's surprise daughter, Sarah Dingwell Peny, arrived from Pittsburgh to introduce herself and apply for the family's support.

When the main rooms of the Second Street house were inventoried in the spring of 1786, they held 41 chairs, and *"10 old mahogany chairs many broke"* were found in the attic. No set of five appears. Ten stood in the front parlor, ten stood in the back (or dining) parlor which connected to a separate kitchen wing, and twelve were in the two large bedrooms. A third and smaller parlor at the foot of the stairs held a mahogany dining table but no chairs. Among the Chippendale pieces inventoried were two marble-top tables for which Wainwright has found evidence that their frames may have come from Randolph's shop. The second Mrs. Cadwalader described these as "the marble sideboards." A silversmith was called in to weigh the plate.

What happened to all these things?

We don't even know how many hairy-paw chairs started out in the Second Street house, and cause will presently appear to suspect the accuracy of "sets" reconstructed from the numbers above. A century later, at any rate, long after the mansion was pulled down and Adams, Randolph, and Randolph's lodger had finished their business in Philadelphia, much of the contents was owned by the General's great-grandson, Dr. Charles E. Cadwalader.

*James Thomas Flexner, *George Washington in the American Revolution* (Boston: Little, Brown, 1967).

Through most of his life Dr. Charles Cadwalader stayed a bachelor, and a very eligible one. Twice he broke engagements to socialites. In 1897, when he was 58, he saw fit to take himself off the market by marrying his housemaid. She was young and Irish, and her name was Bridget Mary Ryan. "Brightie," as she was called below stairs, was a quiet and slender girl; her sense and soft brogue enchanted the Doctor. Several years before, she had crossed the ocean in steerage, leaving six brothers and sisters in Tipperary. Interest in the wedding along Philadelphia's Main Line was not dampened at all by the groom's knack for getting his foot in his mouth. To the press he explained, "With a scientific man's bluntness . . . it was wise to have new and vigorous blood infused into the family." Also, even though the bride's people were now "agriculturists," they came of royal blood in the distant past.

This didn't sit well with the Doctor's brother or the Philadelphia Old Guard.

For a few years the couple stuck it out in Dr. Charles's house on South Fourth Street; then he decided to move to England with his wife. They did so in 1904, but just before they went, the Doctor arranged to leave them all a little something to remember him by. He had nearly the whole contents of the family mansion carted over to Davis & Harvey's on Walnut Street and put on the block. The consignment ran to 358 lots, one of them catalogued as *"Ten Handsome Antique Mahogany Chairs; scroll legs, upholstered in Canary satin damask."* They made $180.* One of the marble-top pier tables brought the auction's top dollar the day before, $450, from the dealer James Curran. It's now in the Metropolitan's American Wing.

Did the five Fanshawes go out here? We didn't know.

When the Charles Cadwaladers sailed for Europe, they took along a chest of family silver but left eighteen portraits in the Historical Society for safekeeping, including five Peales, two Gilbert Stuarts, a Sully, and an Eakins. The Doctor died in London two and a half years later, but Bridget Mary lived on there into the 1950s. She didn't remarry and never returned to Philadelphia. She chose to sign over her portraits not to her brother-in-law but to his son, John Cadwalader, Jr. In the 1930s Bridget Mary sent the silver back to be divided among her husband's great-nephews and nieces. She gave the remaining letters from Washington to General John Cadwalader to the Pennsylvania Historical Society. Apparently she was more of a lady than some of them thought.

* *Philadelphia Evening Bulletin*, November 4, 1904.

This story is fact, but nobody could be sure if it fits.

The Fanshawes might have disappeared, possibly into Wanamaker's, from the fiasco on Walnut Street. If Hanlon worked for the store, why did he misspell his employer's name with two n's? (Because he couldn't spell?)

I dropped a note to John Wanamaker's personnel director asking about Hanlon. My question wasn't that easy, for actually "the store" had and has a number of locations with hundreds of temporary help before Christmas, casuals all the time, and probably furniture repairers called in on contract. I couldn't even give a year. After a month came a reply from the pension administrator—no C. Hanlon had got a pension there. Might Hanlon have been instead a customer?

There were more likely possibilities, among them that the five chairs were not auctioned on November 3–4, 1904. The Doctor might have taken them to London, or maybe he never owned them at all. The sale catalogue describes the consignment as *"choicest specimens of Mahogany Colonial Chairs, Sofas, Sideboard, Tables and Old China, formerly owned by General John Cadwalader, of Revolutionary fame."* Auctioneers dearly love a celebrity, but Wainwright notes that most of the lots actually were never owned by the General. A *Bulletin* reporter invited to the South Fourth Street house at the time of the wedding wrote that many of its furnishings, which included Japanese screens, a stereopticon with one lens gone, tropical plants, and stuffed birds, were collected by Dr. Charles or his mother. Other Cadwaladers held and still hold family heirlooms, including the famed hairy-paw card table.

If the chairs crossed the Atlantic in 1904, at any rate, we'd lost the picture for just thirty years, because in 1934 they reappeared at the country place of Mrs. Nancy Connell.

We can now fade back to our starting point in Major Fanshawe's own words: "My first wife & I inherited St. Catherine's Park, Leixlip (about 10 miles from Dublin) from a very great friend, Mrs. Nancy Connell, about 1952. (Mrs. Connell was a famous Master of the Meath Foxhounds & a sister of Miss Evie Hone who was equally famous for her stained glass & paintings. The large window in Eton College Chapel is her work.) About the early 1920's the late Lord Westmeath was forced to sell his large family estate in Co Westmeath & most of the contents. Much of the furniture was bought by Mrs. Connell. Owing to heavy taxation, & continually forced into ever smaller houses, I had to sell much of my share of the furniture including the 5 chairs. I have never been in contact with the present Ld. Westmeath, but I believe Sotheby's representative, Richard Allen, who started the sale, has. I understand [Lord Westmeath's] ancestors had some American connections. The present owner of St. Catherine's Park (a very fine small Georgian house) is Sir Stafford King Harmon."

Now the chessboard has been turned and the pieces' disposition seems strange. In his book *In Search of Ireland*, writing half a century ago, H. V. Morton gives us at least the scent of Mrs. Connell's world: "In the hotels of Dublin at tea-time enter men in riding-breeches and girls in habits with mud on their boots and wind in the cheeks. In the season they hunt with the Meath of Kildare Hounds and get back to Dublin in time for tea. This nearness to the country and to that abiding passion of the Irish, a horse, is another of Dublin's Georgianisms."

But Major Fanshawe's impression of when and where the chairs passed from Westmeath to his old friend and benefactress Nancy Connell seems mistaken. William A. Nugent, the present Lord Westmeath, lives in England at Bradfield, Reading, Berks. Lately he wrote me of his uncle, the 11th Earl: "I know nothing whatsoever about the Westmeath chairs. . . . The only people who might be able to tell you whether the 11th earl was in USA during 1904 would be the family solicitors, Messrs E & G Stapleton, 31 Kildare Street, Dublin 2. With regard to the estate, this was at PALLAS, TYNAGH, NR LOUGHREA, CO GALWAY. I believe the family left Co Westmeath in Cromwellian time—to Hell or Connaught! Yours faithfully, *Westmeath*"

Galway lies in the province of Connaught. There in the fields of Tynagh township the walls and tower of Pallas Castle still stand, looking not like our pathetic amusement park ones but "marvellous, remote," of wasted stones. Soon after the Irish rebellion of 1641, Cromwell's commissioners, having taken the Nugents' land in County Westmeath, drove them west not to hell but to Connaught, where they were given Pallas with thousands of acres just forfeited by the Burkes. Thomas Burke had backed Charles I against Cromwell's parliament. It was Richard Nugent, 2nd Earl of Westmeath, who signed the articles for the Irish surrender of the province of Leinster. Oliver the Protector himself then wrote urging his supporters to honor the terms (but we're going to leave that right there)!

Some time after 1800 the Nugents built a mansion—a scaled-down Buckingham Palace—next to their Galway castle. They seem to have suffered less in their transplantation than other Catholic landowners.

Their original stake in Ireland came from a grant of "*the lands of Bracklyn*" in Westmeath to Hugh de Nugent, a Norman who died in 1213. Anthony Francis Nugent, 11th Earl, whose dates are 1870–1933, succeeded his father at Pallas when he was a boy of 13. After graduating at Christ Church, Oxford, he served in 1895–97, according to *Burke's Peerage*, as "hon. attaché to H. M. Embassy at Washington." H. M. was still Victoria. What does an honorary attaché do? I asked this question of the British Embassy and David de Boinville there wrote back patiently: "I am unable, I am afraid, to tell you what the Earl of Westmeath's duties here would have been as Honorary Attaché. The staff, as you can see, was extremely small, only 9 people being listed, including the Ambassador! His duties may well have been very varied, no doubt divided between political and social." We see a young man like Captain James Bellamy with money and connections. In fact, Westmeath resigned his unpaid job there not in 1897 but in August 1898, and his next appointment was as assistant private secretary to Joseph Chamberlain in London. Chamberlain was then colonial secretary with two sons, Austen and Neville, also destined for power in the government. De Boinville saw no evidence that Westmeath later returned to the United States, "though, of course, he may have come back at some period on holiday." In 1901 Anthony Nugent was seated in the House of Lords as a Representative Peer for Ireland. (Vacancies in the Lords, Lloyd George complained, were generally filled by chance from among the unemployed!) Nugent's photo taken in robes about then shows he regarded his earldom seriously—he gazes evenly into the 20th century, wearing an ermine-banded coronet, a sword, and knee-breeches. He is a mini-king with a mini-castle standing in his demesne in Galway. The portrait astonishes us for another reason—he looks like John Cadwalader.

There's an innocence about these two that startles and then charms us. When they wanted chairs they would find thrones.

The family solicitor in Dublin didn't wax so lyrical. On December 12, 1933, Lord Westmeath, a bachelor, died of a stroke in the Kildare Street Club, Dublin. His brother Gilbert, succeeding as 12th Earl, ordered the lands in Galway sold, with castle, mansion, and furnishings. This was handled by George Stapleton's firm—actually by his father. On September 16, 1975, he wrote me: "After his Lordship's death his property Pallas Loughrea was sold the following year and we note from our records that in August 1934 we received the proceeds of sale of the furniture at Pallas and we believe the entire contents were sold except for family silver, jewellery and three or four rather valuable pictures. Unfortunately the Writer did not have the pleasure of knowing the late Earl but [from] what we have been told about him and our personal knowledge of the family, we feel quite sure his Lordship would not have disposed of any of his personal chattels in 1920."

The link between Philadelphia and Pallas in Galway remained missing.

Soon after visiting Ron De Silva I mentioned the Cadwalader connection to Berry Tracy, curator in charge of the Metropolitan's American Wing. Tracy said he'd bet that the chair the Met had just purchased from Sack came from the Cadwalader family of Philadelphia. I asked Morrison Heckscher, who's also a curator there, if the price was public. He said not.

"I don't care what you paid for it but some of our readers may."

"That may be *all* they care about it," Heckscher said jovially.

We can all divide 207,500 by 5, and as De Silva had told me to do that, I asked, "How about $41,500 plus Sack's commission?"

Heckscher allowed this to be very near the mark. He handed me a photo of the signature on chair VII, executed in a rather slapdash hand. Nobody had a clue to the signer's identity. I said, "Does that look like 19th-century writing to you?"

"It looks like early 20th-century writing to me," Heckscher said.

Their chair hadn't yet been placed on view but was in conservation. They were putting a seat in it. Tracy and Heckscher led the way to their workshop in the museum's basement. It looked nearly as hard to crack as the vault at Fort Knox. It was locked even with the shop people inside. When they opened the door, I finally saw Fanshawe chair VII. It sat up on the bench stripped clean of upholstery and clamped in several places. After the frame, which had been riddled by tacks, was secure, a new seat would be put in, stuffed and covered. The splat shoe lay on the bench and on tilting it to the light we could read its penciled inscription. With the shoe screwed in place the writing would lie on the upholstery unseen.

Heckscher invited my attention to the splat, a surreal tree of a thing. The mahogany's grain ran vertically up to the four branches that spread to the backrails, but the grain of the branches was laid horizontally for strength. These parts, really thick, were shaped in a tapered section so they look light. How their maker pieced them together was talked over for a couple of minutes by the two curators and a shop man. The shop man got in the last word. It brought to mind a saying of Herbert Cescinsky that the untechnical expert is a contradiction in terms.

We went back up the stairs and passed through the crowd in the lobby. To give the Met's curators their due, they had dug with care before taking a position. Long before I did, they heard from Major Fanshawe that his chairs came from Lord Westmeath. They were ringing Ron De Silva even before Sack came in to make the deal.

The travels of Fanshawe chair VII seemed to be over.

Out on the sidewalk Berry Tracy said he might give one of the research fellows at the museum a little project:

Who was C. Hanlon?

This question also seemed to be left:

Did only five chairs go to Ireland?

2
Pallas

> . . . Ireland, Ireland that cloud in the West, that coming storm . . .
> —Gladstone to his wife, 1845

ONE DAY IN OCTOBER, after packing notes, Xerox prints of the second sample chair, and travel documents, I went down to Kennedy Airport and boarded an Aer Lingus flight for Shannon and Dublin. Stapleton, the solicitor, knew I was coming; he said they'd look for records of the 1934 Pallas sale.

The advantages of flying Irish seem to be, first, it's one of the few transatlantic carriers that gets into Dublin, and second, you feel like you're there when you take your seat. The stewardesses were turned out in smartly tailored green, and the whole crew came on delighted with us and their American equipment, which happened to be a pretty old airplane.

"Is this a DC3?"

"Ah, it's a 707!" our girl sang softly.

The old tank drilled through the night, and a very short night, as if it knew the way. In my raincoat was stuck a paperback guidebook called *Ireland on $10 a Day*, which I took down and studied as the evening wore on. I can't even stay home on $10 a day. (Actually, it's no trick to see any country on this amount—you just don't eat, drink, sleep, or move.)

The next afternoon I stood on rubbery legs looking up Kildare Street. E. & G. Stapleton, Solicitors and Land Agents, occupied a Georgian house of mud-colored brick halfway up the row. Possibly tenants paid their rents downstairs, since the waiting room was fenced in two by a counter. I was shown up a flight of stairs to the solicitor's office, a dark room filled with oil portraits and the heavy furniture of an earlier time. Stapleton rose and shook hands, a tall, urbane man, his hair just starting gray and worn long, either because the fashion had reached Dublin or because it never left. I asked if he was "E" or "G." "Neither one!" he said. He was George S., but others in the family had supplied the founders' initials.

I told him what I hoped to find. Not the missing hairy-paw chairs, although that would be nice. If they hadn't been broken up long ago for firewood, they were more likely over here than in Philadelphia. But I don't go around trying to win the Irish Sweepstakes, and Major Fanshawe had already done that. I passed Stapleton a Xerox print of the Winterthur sample. Could he tell me who the 1934 auctioneer was?

"Battersby, Upper Fitzwilliam Road."

Stapleton's firm received the sale proceeds on August 14, 1934. He said the furniture at Pallas netted £1,556 and its library £245. Presumably that left out Westmeath's art, silver, glass, china, and oddments. Even in that depression year, the property must have brought many times more than the contents.

"Do you have the estate inventory?"

No, it was gone. And personally he'd had nothing to do with handling his Lordship's estate. He knew only the present Earl, whose father and uncle had been served by *his* father. Stapleton regarded me genially but with care. It was clear all this dredging presented him with a problem that might pose some awkward features.

"Does anyone here remember the 11th Earl?"

"No."

"There must be somebody—a relative, an old servant?"

He thought they would be gone by now. Even the mansion was pulled down.

"But why?"

"Nobody wanted them, really."

Even today the neoclassical houses continue to go down, though in Britain at least they seem to be graded on their merits and sometimes are boarded up by borough councils that are nearly as broke as their former occupants.

Stapleton offered a cigarette and lit one himself. He said, "We have found one thing."

He handed over an old ledger. On its title page was entered in ink: *Inventory and Valuation Conducted at Pallas—Bennett & Son, Valuers, 6 Upper Ormond Quay, Dublin—November 1913.*

"*Lovely!*"

"In it there seems to be only this . . . "

He showed me a page of handwriting. One line read: *13 Mahogany Chairs carved frames & seats, covered in leather cloth. . . . £26 5/s.*

The leather cloth sounded unattractive and unlikely, and thirteen chairs just too many. Only five, in any case, came out of St. Catherine's Park.

"A set of five here someplace?"

He shook his head; this was the news he had for me.

Stapleton mentioned the name *David Hone*, a kin of Mrs. Connell's. Hone still lived in Dublin over on Lower Baggot Street. "He might start you in a new direction," Stapleton suggested. He flipped open the telephone directory and told me Hone's number. (One book does for all Ireland!)

"First I need to go through this line by line," I said of the ledger.

"You won't find them there."

"Well, here is an entry, *American Organ in Walnut Case by Esty Organ Co. . . . £12.* Other American items may tell us something."

He took me to a downstairs room and left me with the ledger. In a bold and faultless hand it recited the contents of Pallas just before World War I, down to the furnishings of the butler's room, servants' hall, carpenter shop, and stable. A full-length portrait by Sir Peter Lely of Lord Riverston, a 17th-century Chief Justice of Ireland, had hung over the chimney piece in the mansion's hall. Other Lely portraits of James II and of his queen, more pictures, furniture, glass, porcelain, silver, books, Irish manuscripts. . . . Bennett must have been out there for days. No item besides the Esty organ was called American. In addition to the thirteen banquet chairs just one other set was listed: *4 Carved Mahogany Chairs. . . . £8 8/s.* The ledger's grand total added to £9,058.

George Stapleton had offered no opinion, a detail I appreciated. Possibly it was not his clients who missed the boat, but me.

In a chill drizzle that alternated with thin sunshine, I walked back up Kildare Street, over the River Liffey on O'Connell Bridge, and into O'Connell Street, the Broadway of Dublin. My bed-and-breakfast house wasn't up there but the Gresham Hotel was, with heat in it, pots of tea, and sandwiches. From the lobby, I phoned David Hone. He sounded like an aristocrat and a jolly one. He knew of no chairs at Leixlip. No, and he barely remembered Nancy Hone Connell.

"Well, she knew her antiques," I said lamely.

"Ah, she knew how to fall off a horse!"

Hone said I might like to look up a Mr. Leo Smith at the Dawson Gallery in Dawson Street. At one time Smith was Evie Hone's business agent. Hadn't he managed to sell some of her art to her sister, Nancy Connell? Smith must have been to St. Catherine's Park in those days. I thanked Hone and hung up.

The lounge of the Gresham held no girls in habit with wind in their cheeks, but there was one in a pants suit I'd seen by the Aer Lingus counter at Kennedy the day before. The waiter brought tea in a plated pot, a heap of little sandwiches, and cheerful but not so simple instructions on how to reach Dawson Street.

The gallery was on the second floor and Leo Smith happened to be in, a silver-haired man with the indoor look of dealers everywhere. He glanced at the Xerox print. Yes, he had called on Nancy Connell back in the fifties. He might well have sat on such a chair at St. Catherine's Park or one quite like it. That was what she cared about, antiques. The house had been full of them. She'd taken from him a few pictures painted by her sister Evie, but art wasn't so much Mrs. Connell's thing. When it came to money, the Hones had plenty. Unless he was mistaken, hadn't Nancy Connell's money come from the Clyde? He'd heard her speak of Mrs. Fanshawe, the first one. She wanted the Fanshawes to have St. Catherine's Park when she was gone, to keep it intact. Instead, when they got it they parted and sold the place. As for the chair, he might just have seen it there and he might not have. Well, that was what she cared about, antiques.

After thanking Leo Smith, I went looking for Battersby & Co. on Upper Fitzwilliam Road. "Roads" run all through the city; Fitzwilliam was around the corner of Dawson Street, past St. Stephen's Green, and two blocks down. Battersby has been in business for a century and a half and is on a modest scale the Sotheby's of Dublin. But I was told Mr. Judd, the boss, was engaged. Tomorrow after eleven would be better.

After dinner at Jurys Hotel in Ballsbridge, its lounge was full of American husbands and wives cocktailing. They were travel agents from Boston! Jurys is a chain with other hotels in Limerick, Cork, Westport, and Sligo. The Dublin one had tourist shops and a cabaret offering in season Irish music, dancing, and storytelling, which Dubliners call "export entertainment." The Dubliners were more likely tuned to BBC, catching Woody Herman or other *Big Bands at the Dorchester*. The only export entertainments they seem to inflict on themselves are newscasts in Irish, which nobody understands. Here turned their curious agony. Before Yeats put plays like *Cathleen ni Houlihan* on the boards of his new national theater, he once went to a Masonic concert at Sligo, but he would have none of it: "Somebody sang a stage Irishman's song—the usual whiskey, shillelagh kind of thing—and I hissed him, and lest my hiss might be lost in the general applause, waited until the applause had died down and hissed again. That gave somebody else also courage, and we both hissed."

The quilt (or "rug") on the bed was overstuffed like a kapok raft and too small, so it kept sliding off. I lay there freezing and trying to balance the rug. Through the curtains across the road loomed the lighted ramparts of the American Embassy with an art-deco eagle fixed on them. If you should ever lie cold in Dublin, a hell of a lot of good the American Embassy will do you!

At Battersby the next morning, Noel Judd remembered nothing of the Pallas sale; in 1934 he, too, had been a child. His father Raymond Judd was auctioneer then, and many of the old records got destroyed a few years ago when the business was moved from Westmoreland Street.

"You don't have a catalogue, or maybe your old invoices?"

"I'm afraid not."

"Did you run ads, say, in *Country Life?*"

"They would be in *The Irish Times* and *Independent.* My school, Trinity, keeps copies; also the National Library."

Judd was cordial and polished, a Trinity College man on his surface much like Stapleton. Trinity is the Ivy League of Ireland. It is planted in Dublin's center like Yale in New Haven's, and its undergraduates, too, go around dressed like bums! Judd promised to have his records looked through, but the prospects there didn't look good.

An hour later I sat winding microfilms of the *Irish Independent* in the National Library on Kildare Street. If you have to go into newspaper files without a date, you're dead, but these we had. Anthony Nugent died December 12, 1933; his solicitors got the proceeds of sale the next August 14. That should put the auction in June or July. Sure enough, the reel stopped on June 19:

BATTERSBY'S AUCTIONS
Sale today and following days at 12 o'clock
"Pallas", Loughrea
By direction of the Rt. Hon. Earl of Westmeath

THE ANTIQUE AND MODERN FURNITURE OF THE MANSION
Admission to view & sale by ticket only, 1/
Battersby & Co., Auctioneers & Valuers
39 Westmoreland St., Dublin
Established 1815

This we mostly had. The question was whether the *Independent* had followed up with a news story. Here good luck; it ran the next day, June 20:

SALE AT EARL'S GALWAY HOME

Many Buyers Present

The sale at the seat of the Earl of Westmeath at Pallas, Co. Galway, was opened yesterday by Messrs. Battersby & Co., auctioneers, Dublin, and attracted a very large attendance. Buyers were present from Galway and adjoining counties, Dublin, Belfast, Cork, London and Paris. Buying was brisk throughout.

. . . A set of mahogany dining tables brought £16. A double carved mahogany oval sideboard, with lofty mirror back, was bought for 25 guineas, and a rosewood bookcase and cabinet for 10½ guineas. Five dining room chairs fetched £19. . . .

Ah, did they now! Balboa could not have gazed on the Pacific with more pleasure!

From the gloom this nearly forgotten peer and his Philadelphia chairs were going to emerge. Bennett appraised no set of five at Pallas in 1913, so these had not likely descended in the family. Nor apparently could Westmeath have bought them in 1904. The *Independent* petered out the next day with a follow-up ad: "Sale today of THE VALUABLE LIBRARY OF BOOKS." *The Irish Times* carried the same item as the *Independent* on the first day's bidding, and on June 23 picked up the bedroom furniture:

FURNITURE AT PALLAS SOLD

From Our Correspondent
LOUGHREA, Friday

> **The furnishings of the principal bedrooms were disposed of today at the auction by Battersby & Co., Dublin, at Pallas, County Galway, the seat of the Earl of Westmeath. There was again a large attendance . . .**

I took a break in the courtyard and another one in the Library's monumental Victorian W.C. downstairs, then went back to the desk and drew an earlier reel—obits this time.

The Irish Times, December 13, 1933:

> THE EARL OF WESTMEATH
>
> We regret to announce that the Earl of Westmeath died early this morning at the Kildare Street Club, Dublin.
>
> The Right Honourable Anthony Francis Nugent, eleventh Earl of Westmeath, was an Irish Representative Peer. He was born on January 11, 1870 and succeeded his father in 1883. He was educated at Christ Church, Oxford, where he graduated in 1895. In 1902 he was appointed a Senator of the Royal University of Ireland, which conferred on him the honorary degree of LL.D. seven years later.
>
> The late Earl was Honorary Attaché to the British Embassy in Washington from 1895 until 1897, and in the following year was appointed Secretary of the Royal Commission which was set up to inquire into the French treaty rights in Newfoundland. Later in the same year he became Assistant Private Secretary to the Secretary of State for the Colonies, the Rt. Hon. Joseph Chamberlain, M.P., a post which he held until 1901, when he was elected a Representative Peer for Ireland. He was also a Justice of the Peace and a Deputy Lieutenant for Galway, where he had his seat at Pallas, Loughrea. In 1921 he was appointed a Privy Councillor.
>
> The Earl of Westmeath was a member of the Carlton, Wellington, County (Galway) and Kildare Street Clubs.
>
> The Earl had a severe stroke on Sunday last, and was being cared for at the Club, Kildare Street. His brother, the Hon. Gilbert Charles Nugent, who succeeds to the Earldom, was born in 1880. . . .

A few days later *The Times* reported that the Earl's body was taken by hearse to Galway, where the funeral mass was said in Tynagh Church. It was then placed in

> the family vault in the ancient ruins of the Dominican Monastery at Kilcorban.
>
> Chief mourners were the Hon. Gilbert C. Nugent, Messrs. James & Henry Smith, Masonbrook, the Duc de Stacpool, and Major Smith.
>
> Among the general public were Dr. A. Comyn, Mr. C. O'Farrell, Dalystown, Captain B. Daly and Mrs. Daly, Brig-Gen. Hickie and

brother, Captain Gough, Mr. J. D. O'Kelly, Mr. Horner, Mr. C. G. Stapleton and Mr. Hamilton.

Wreaths were sent by Lady Emily, the Pallas employés . . .

The mourners looked interesting, though it seemed unlikely any of them still lived. C. G. Stapleton I recognized first. The Duke de Stacpool wrote a popular book about the hunting life, *Irish and Other Memories*, in 1881; possibly this mourner was his son. Who was Lady Emily, and why hadn't she come herself?

That week an early portrait of Anthony Nugent ran centered on *The Times's* picture page, surrounded by shots of Irish Free State Girl Guides, a rugby trial, and two girls in mid-calf-length dresses rehearsing the parts of Robin Hood and Maid Marion for a pantomime at the Gaiety Theatre. At first it looked as if Nugent too must be rehearsing a part, for he wears an ermine cape, ermine-banded coronet, knee breeches, and dress sword. No, he is in robes, and the portrait, although undated, probably has to do with his being seated in the Lords as a peer in 1901. (Lord Randolph Churchill as Chancellor of the Exchequer also turned out in full dress on occasion, and complained bitterly when his successor refused to buy his kit.) Here Nugent makes a handsome peer. That he never found his countess seems curious, and this in turn must have led to his fading with such remarkable speed from the memory of Ireland, his solicitors, and even his family.

It was time to leave Dublin and try my luck at Pallas. First I'd go to Galway City and ask the editors of the local paper to help me shake the tree.

The kitchen and dining room of that Ballsbridge guesthouse were where the heat was—who heats a bedroom in Ireland? For breakfast, just before train time, boiled eggs, oatmeal, toast, marmalade, even fair coffee, and across the uncrowded room at this time came a pretty and delicate girl with big lavender eyes. She sat down by me and chatted, because it was the friendly thing to do. She was an art history student from Limerick. Just what was I doing in Ireland? *Researching antiques?*

"My father collects antiques! Sheraton pieces mostly."

"Yes, well, that's a fun way to stay broke."

"Oh, he isn't broke. He found a walnut table for £14."

"Irish Sheraton?"

"No, *walnut*!"

She ate her toast. I felt like a complete cluck. Walnut isn't a Sheraton wood but belongs to the Queen Anne period nearly a century earlier.

"I'll be entering Trinity," she whispered, "but first I must find a flat...."

"You'll find one."

"It's not easy to find a flat in Dublin!"

Some day she might be just a sorrowful madonna with hemorrhoids, but now she came on with those unbelievable eyes, lavender—or was her sweater lavender? The taxi was outside for Heuston Station in Kingsbridge.

And now when I couldn't take any notes came the memorable cab driver.

He was a big prizefighter and eager to oblige. The heavy bag meant nothing to him. Had he emigrated a hundred years before, he'd have driven spikes for the Union Pacific! The problem right now was to get stamps for my postcards. He pulled up across from an Office (post-office), and shouted:

"Stay put, you'll be killed in the fooking traffic!"

He danced over to the Office, then back daintily holding the stamps and little *Par Avion* stickers to go with them. I thanked him for this courtesy. The Dublin traffic *was* murder. Would it be a good idea to rent a car in Galway? Well, yes and no.

"Every car they let to a Yank they should mark on the top YANK DRIVING! Like a driving school, you see, nothing personal. Them French, too. YANK or FRENCH DRIVING! Then we know to stay out of their fooking way! Now I'm going to tell you what to do. Make a nice sign for yesself, and you write on it KEEP LEFT!"

"And put that on the roof?"

"No, no, right here! Put it over the cowl, you see? It's for your own welfare I'm telling you. Now tell me, did you get on at Mrs. ———?"

"Yes, except I froze my ass off."

"Ah, she runs a nice house. Her daughters was Aer Lingus stewardesses, they married doctors. Glamor girls, them stewardesses!"

At the station he danced out with the bag. "Take what you need," I said, holding out a pile of coins—new Irish, old Irish, and English sterling. He picked at them with care.

"*You want money in this country, be a doctor! God bless ye!*"

The train for Tullamore, Ballinasloe, and Galway crossed the country in about three hours, a diesel-electric as clean as a whistle. It clattered along, scattering sheep with red and blue paint marks on their buttocks

CIVIL SERVICE DANCE.—The committee and some of their guests at the da
at the Metropole Ballroom, Dublin. Included are Mr. J. Gonner, Mr. V. N.
Mr. J. J. Barry, Mrs. Malone, Mrs. Kiely, Miss Bruen, Mrs. Gorman, Mr.

RUGBY TRIAL.—A line-out in
Whites'" match yesterday at
rbrook, Dublin.

An early portrait of the Earl of Westmeath, whose death has been announced.

IRISH FREE STATE GIRL GUIDES' ME
ing in the Mansion House, Dublin, yesterd
(left) and Mrs. M.

PANTOMIME.—Miss Cora Goffin, who plays "Robin Hood," and Miss Seymour ("Maid Marion"), rehearsing yesterday for the Gaiety Theatre, Dublin, Pantomime, "The Babes in the Wood."

Anthony Francis Nugent, 11th Earl of Westmeath

—*Irish Times,* Dublin, December 15, 1933

but not getting much notice from the cattle. This was the plain of Leinster, the fertile midlands, changing around halfway to Connaught province. It was hard to believe thousands once starved here. My heart leapt at the first Norman fortifications drawing up to the train window, but the ramparts turned out to be those of a modern sewage treatment plant. For shame, Galway Bay, too, has been oversold—you have to bring the song with you:

> If you ever go across the sea to Ireland,
> Then maybe at the closing of your day
> You will sit and watch the moon rise over Claddagh,
> And see the sun go down on Galway Bay.

The bay we passed was just gray ocean beating on the rocks. At Galway City the CIE terminal deadends into the rear of the Great Southern Hotel, built of huge stone blocks. The Great Southern opened in 1856 together with transatlantic steamer service between Galway and St. John's, Newfoundland, via the Atlantic Royal Mail Line.

The town surrounds an ancient green, Eyre Square. A few years ago, they got carried away and changed its name to John F. Kennedy Square, but it didn't take. This was like trying to get New Yorkers to call Sixth Avenue the Avenue of the Americas. I checked into the Odeon, a small and busy hotel on the green with a bar and tearoom on its street floor. Then I went looking for *The Connacht Tribune*. (*Connacht* is Irish for *Connaught,* and they both say *kŏn′ot.*)

Two of the paper's editors, Sean Fahy and John Conningham, listened to my story, and Fahy agreed to find a photographer for the trip to Tynagh next morning. Fahy had been to Pallas once, but Conningham never heard of it. The castle stands about 30 miles east of Galway City, off the back road between Tynagh and Portumna. Tourists, and apparently natives, didn't often get there. Pallas isn't mentioned in Fodor's *Guide*.

We picked up Westmeath's obituary on *The Tribune*'s microfilm, which added a few details:

> The Barony of Devlin, which he held, was an ancient Irish title. . . . He was a Catholic and a bachelor. . . . The late Earl of Westmeath was a man of simple disposition and a great employer of labour. He sold the greater portion of his property over 20 years ago to the Land Commission, when it was converted into new farms and parcelled out amongst the uneconomic holders on the estate. He . . . continually kept a staff of about 40

> workmen, who were very much attached to their employer. Not alone did he retain the old employees, but he was continually taking on additional ones. Recently he expended many thousands of pounds on improvements in the residence and surroundings.

The paper then told of an incident during the Troubles. One day his Lordship "utilized a push-bicycle" (i.e., rode a bike) on some errand or other. The constables mistook him for an insurgent, but he wasn't long in setting them straight.

The auction items also added a little. Again "*Five dining room chairs fetched £19.*" Although bidding on the furniture was termed "keen," it turned slow on the books "except for Irish manuscripts." When the hammer fell for the last time on Friday, June 22, 1934, the Reverend Mr. P. J. O'Loughlin proposed "a vote of thanks to Messrs. Battersby for the courteous and able manner in which the sale was conducted, and the vote of thanks passed by acclamation." Judd had already sold the real estate separately:

> A sale of the property has been arranged by Messrs. Battersby. The demesne embraces close on 1,000 acres with a magnificent mansion house, near which is situated the ruins of the old castle dating back to the 14th Century, and considered by archaeologists to be in the best state of preservation of any of its kind.

Yes, we could see the boxy old cars drawn up to the mansion, the dealers' vans from Dublin and Belfast, the picnic hampers, whispered strategies for bidding. The cottagers and servants must have known for months that the game was up at Pallas, and Gilbert Nugent had before now taken away the portraits by Lely. What brought Mrs. Connell this June week from the other side of Ireland? Maybe simple collector's fever, or possibly the fact that the nearby cathedral, St. Brendan's in Loughrea, just had put in some stained-glass windows by Evie Hone. To Nancy Connell had the thirteen banquet chairs made too big a lot—too many for these days, just as the house was too big and hopelessly remote? Anthony Nugent himself must have discarded the prospect of taking his meals in that array of mahogany, or why had he returned one day from parts unknown with a set of five? Now these would be right for St. Catherine's Park.

That evening the paper's photographer Stan Shields called from the hotel desk and we went into the bar to have a drink and talk it over. Shields proved good news—a native Galwegian, short, husky, and professionally indifferent to storm or mist. "If I can see it I can shoot it." He came just now from shooting a Romanian cargo ship of some 3,000 tons, one of the largest vessels ever to call at Galway. Besides working for *The Tribune* he covered racing, rugby, and other sports in the west as a stringer for the Dublin papers. Pallas and its chairs were news to him, as they had been to Conningham.

In the morning we checked out a rented Fiat and headed east on the main road for Loughrea. Shields drove—it's one thing to keep left and it's something else in that dreamy land to do intersections with pedestrians and road signs in Irish. The country turned out to be smooth sailing, not quite flat but with a groundswell to it. As back in Connecticut, the rocks of glacial till had long ago—much longer ago—been laid up into walls, though they looked different, usually broken to make smooth faces and piled higher. The air was cool and moist, an overcast floating in from the west. If you put it all together it spelled *foxhunt*.

We weren't long in coming on one. The fox and pack were gone, but two hunters sat their mounts reined in by the road and a girl stood on the wall scanning the horizon. They seem to do quite a bit of scanning the horizon in that sport, as in sailboat racing. It may be a patrician's sport, but in Ireland almost everybody who can climb or be pushed up onto a nag—kids, priests, and septuagenarians—goes after the fox. They say the fox nearly always gets away.

A few miles beyond Loughrea we took a right onto the back road for Tynagh village. This is the kind of road that doesn't need a Cadillac, hard-surfaced but squeezed and blinded by walls and hedgerows. The village proved hard to find; Tynagh is more a township and parish—the old word is *barony*—of range and farmland. After a while, as no battlements materialized on our right, we stopped and asked an old man in a torn black suit, who tottered over to the Fiat.

"Eh, Pallas? Done and gone! Gone! Gone!"

We thanked him and went on.

"Jesus, it's supposed to be in the best shape of any castle in Galway!"

"Let me do the asking," Shields said.

A few houses on, a young fellow came out and Shields said something like, "Good morning! Good morning, sir! We are hoping to find Pallas Castle in this direction. I'm wondering could you be of assistance to us?"

"This is it! Down the lane there!"

Shields turned right into the lane, and then the brown crenellated walls and tower of Pallas appeared, riding far off in the grass like an abandoned ship. It seemed a long way from the Second Street townhouse of John Cadwalader, and the Nugents' mansion, too, was done and gone, as the old man meant. We pulled up by its foundation wall and got out. A stone cottage—the old gardener's cottage—stood between the empty foundation and the castle gate. A small dog came yipping, then the caretaker stepped out of the cottage, a tall, spare man in his eighties. The overcast had blown our way.

Shields managed the introductions. The keeper's name was Francis Martyn. I got it only with difficulty and doubt if he got ours. He took us through the gate of the keep, over which was inset a slab bearing the coronet and arms, apparently of Riverston, and incised: *1719* . . . [illegible] . . . *DEO ET FIDELLS.**

Rather than plunging into the esoterica of Norman castles, I've put at the back of this book an appreciation of Pallas written in 1908 by J. P. Dalton of the Galway Archaeological and Historical Society. Besides sorting out the Nugents and Burkes, Dalton's is the only account I've ever found of a visit to the 11th Earl at home.

In the bawn, or courtyard, a plaque was mounted by the tower door:

> *This is one of the best preserved castles of its type in the county, with both its tower and bawn in a good state of preservation. It was built by the Burkes around 1500, and in 1574 was in the hands of Jonyck FitzThomas Burke. During the Cromwellian period it was assigned to the Nugents, Earls of Westmeath, in whose hands it remained until recently.*

Inside the tower door I started up a spiral stairway of cut stone. Its risers were steeper than on our modern iron ones and its treads slippery—many a man-at-arms must have come down here on his back! Dalton writes that in his day the second floor was of wicker, "made by weaving tough ashen twigs in basket fashion through the joists; and, on

*Pallas in 1719 was the seat of the 2nd Lord Riverston, a Nugent. After the Restoration Richard Nugent, the 2nd Earl of Westmeath, had left Galway and returned to his lands in County Westmeath. He gave Pallas to Thomas, his second son. The Burkes never got it back. Thomas Nugent rose in 1687 to become Lord Chief Justice of the King's Bench in Dublin, and in 1689 was created Baron Riverston. The Chief Justice, whose portrait by Lely had hung in the mansion hall, seems not to have been highly regarded as a jurist. The Oxford *Dictionary of National Biography* says "Nugent's demeanour on the bench was not dignified, and we are told that in a charge to the Dublin grand jury he expressed a hope that William's followers [i.e., supporters of the Protestant William III] would soon be 'hung up all over England' in 'bunches like a rope of onions'." By mid-19th century the family branch in County Westmeath lapsed into extinction. This enabled the then Lord Riverston at Pallas to drop that later title, becoming instead 9th Earl of Westmeath. His name was Anthony Francis Nugent and his grandson, named for him, became the 11th Earl.

Tower and bawn, Pallas Castle
—photo by Stan Shields

Slab bearing arms of Lord Riverston (?) at Pallas Castle
—photo by Stan Shields

Francis Martyn at Pallas, October 1975
—photo by Stan Shields

the same story, a wicker door similarly wrought on a wooden frame leads to one of the side cellars." The topmost story but one held the hall—the only space lighted by windows rather than slits. The parapet above, like that over the gate to the keep, was pierced by an open hatch called a machicolation, for dropping things ("stone, boiling water . . . lead" or perhaps just garbage) on unannounced callers. Both these conveniences together with the arms (of Riverston?) were set slightly off center for some reason.

Who built this place and why?

A Norman baron of the De Burgo line built it. Most of these knights and adventurers came not from Normandy but from Wales. In taking over Connaught starting in the 13th century, they were armed with grants and charters from Henry III and later English sovereigns, but the native Irish chiefs hadn't signed any charters, if they could write at all. They fought for their land, they fought one another, their daughters married Anglo-Normans, and by the time Cromwell landed in Dublin, the Nugents and Burkes must have been more Irish than Norman. The 11th Earl's mother had been a Galway girl, Emily Blake, from Furbough in Connemara. When the power of the old Milesian kings had been broken and their lands forfeited, they became specters that never died. Cecil Woodham-Smith writes in *The Great Hunger*: "Until the famine, it was by no means uncommon for poor peasants living in mud cabins to make wills bequeathing estates which had long ago been confiscated from their forefathers, and that figure of fun in Victorian days, the Irish beggar who claimed to be descended from kings, was very often speaking the truth." Bridget Ryan in Philadelphia remembered, too.

By Cromwell's time, the Norman fortifications were going down under the nuclear bomb of its day, the siege gun. Here we go to a book, *Irish Castles*, by H. G. Leask, published by Dundalgan Press, Ltd., Dundalk, 1951: "The advent of gunpowder and artillery rang the death knell of castles . . . " When siege guns were brought up "castle and town wall went down in rubbish beneath the deadly strokes of the cannon and great masses of masonry were rent apart and laid low by a few barrels of gunpowder. . . . Essex, in 1599, besieged and battered Cahir Castle with his heavy guns and, later still, the siege train of Cromwell's army—the heaviest guns brought into the country up to that time—pulverized the stone walls of more than one city." But for most castles, "their tale of ruin was long drawn out—a story of neglect by owners and spoliation by them or the other quarriers of later times. Most of them are roofless and

Francis Martyn at Pallas, October 1975
—photo by Stan Shields

abandoned and a prey to the clinging ivy, destructive green mantle beloved of the sentimentalist."

The siege guns didn't get Pallas, but a quarrier got some and his name seems to have been Nugent. The mansion was partly built of dressed stones taken from the castle and medieval manor house that once abutted its wall.

Francis Martyn showed us the malt house standing by the tower, but it wasn't easy to understand him. Its shell looked like a stone incinerator that had burned wood or peat. Apparently neither the Anglo-Normans nor the Irish went without their ale. Who else held Pallas?

"The militry monks was here," Martyn said.

"*Military monks*? I never heard of any military monks!"

"Blunderbusses they used. They was the same order as the Friars of Loughrea."

Though possibly he had suffered a stroke at some time, Martyn was perfectly sharp. Shields and I considered taking pictures outside the wall—of what, stones? By now I knew Martyn was more important. Shields asked him to pose; he was ready to oblige. The lens looked at him and he looked at the lens. How long had he been there? He was at Pallas 84 years. He had known the 11th Earl, then?

"I worked for his Lordship and the Countess—worked for them till they was gone!"

"Lady Emily was the Countess?"

"His mother the Countess! Lady Emily was his sister! And for Gilbert I worked, he came from Flower Hill."

It was raw and wet and Martyn was cold standing in the bawn. He had difficulty speaking but not thinking. Even when I understood him, it was hard to take notes. Only Shields kept warm, moving around with his Rolleiflex. We would have to come back another day.

Martyn followed us to the red Fiat and shook hands. His little dog yelped when he tried to get her into the cottage. They had seen plenty of us come and go.

We drove to Tynagh Church, not expecting that Father O'Loughlin might still be there but because parish priests are supposed to know everything. In fact, the old church itself was gone, replaced by a new one along the lines of a Holiday Inn. Its pastor suggested we might contact Father P. K. Egan in Portumna, who knew a good bit more than he about local history. I expressed appreciation and got up but Stan

Shields stayed seated, making small talk. It seemed to say, "Forgive us now, Father, he's a Yank!"

Portumna looked to be more of a town than Tynagh, astride a road junction on the bank of the Shannon. Luckily, Father Egan chanced to be in his parish house; he and Shields had met before. He offered us a smoke and then lit one. But forty years was a long time; he hadn't known the Nugents or ever heard of their chairs. Father Egan did recall something about Pallas in the Galway Archaeological Journal—perhaps back in the twenties or thirties? It had a photograph of the mansion. We might look that up. (It's the 1908 piece excerpted in Appendix 1). Had we visited Flower Hill? The Nugents had that once. Its new owner still kept a lovely place there. He couldn't be sure now of his name.

After Shields indicated it was time to go, Father Egan followed us out and asked if there might be a spare snapshot of the chairs. I was pleased to pass him a Xerox print.

Now that the photographs were taken, the sun came out; we barreled down the highway to Loughrea, Galway, and dinner.

What had we got?

A witness, maybe. One thing I've learned about legwork is that witnesses, when you get them, don't often say what you hope they will. When you've looked everywhere for A, you may be lucky enough to find AB+4=X. The thing is to let the equation unfold. Next morning, a Sunday, I inked on the map "KEEP LEFT!", as advised in Dublin, and stuck it over the dash. After a considerable delay while I hunted for the Fiat's choke, the small machine started and rolled out of town without further protest. Stan Shields had already brought unfinished prints to the Hotel Odeon, and on Monday would call the county librarian about the Archaeological Society piece which I needed to photocopy.

Tynagh Church looked well filled, with more bicycles than cars in its yard. Martyn evidently hadn't got there, for when I knocked at the cottage and asked for him, his son, or grandson, let me into the kitchen. Mrs. Martyn was there, completely unlike her husband—small, plump, and wearing glasses. She accepted a print Shields had made of him at the tower. Her kitchen, crowded by a big cast iron stove, made me think of my grandmother's under the Second Avenue el tracks in Yorkville long ago. Mrs. Martyn had worked in the mansion as a housemaid.

Martyn came in as if he'd expected me. Maybe he did. Now the house.

. . . The Red Lord built part of it—helped himself to stones from the castle. Because his hair was red, they called him the Red Lord! In those days the castle gate was of timber with spike-heads in it—never saw that gate, they burned it! Who bought the estate from Battersby? It was sold to a man, he wanted to put a school here. Claffey, was that his name? Then the priest was against it, and nothing came of that. In the end the place was let go to the county, then the Land Commission took it. The house was pulled down, yes.

I picked up my envelope from the kitchen table and showed Martyn a Xerox of the second sample chair. (I had no print of the Fanshawes.)

"Have you seen that before?"

He looked at it.

"*It* was his Lordship's! In the house."

"How many of them?"

When he shook his head I handed the print to Mrs. Martyn.

"Remember them?"

"His Lordship's, yes," she said.

"But there were thirteen chairs covered with leather in the dining room?"

Yes, but these chairs stood in the house. They couldn't say how many or in which room they were. Martyn recalled that his Lordship added two rooms—one an office, the other he didn't know. There had been other improvements such as new masonry. In those years Martyn worked outside and in, as a handyman.

What of the Countess of Westmeath? Might it be she, a widow from 1883, raising her children here, sending her eldest son away to Oxford and the foreign service, who had ruled Pallas all along, since he never brought home a wife?

No, he was *always* gone, and she, too! The agent looked to things. Where they went he couldn't say. Only summers they came with Lady Emily, and they would come for the hunting. Lady Emily. Yes, she was a hunter and horsewoman, a fine looking girl. Married Major Humphreys. The Countess was living when they married. Then Gilbert went to the war, he lived at Flower Hill.

Gilbert Nugent never entered the foreign service but in 1914 went as a major, Royal Artillery, to France, where he was twice wounded. Flower Hill remained the seat of the younger sons. It too was a Riverston house. Charles Anthony Nugent, second son of the 9th Earl, lived there in the later 19th century. In time the place became his nephew Gilbert's. Gilbert sold it after the war, then in 1934 he sold Pallas too.

So he never was master here?

"Gilbert was here! He come here when his Lordship died."

After the December funeral, then, the new 12th Earl moved into Pallas and readied the estate for sale the next summer. And Martyn remembered them all.

"Yes, his Lordship, the Countess, Lady Emily, Gilbert . . . I knew them. . . ."

Martyn's recollection of the man Lady Emily married in 1902 has proved accurate; he is given in *Burke's Peerage* as "Brig. Gen. Gardiner Humphreys, C.B., C.M.G., D.S.O., R.A." And the Countess *was* alive then. She died in 1906. In fact, she raised three sons and several daughters before the turn of the century. Gilbert was her third son. Her second, William Andrew, was cited for gallantry in France as a captain, 15th Hussars, dying in May 1915 of wounds received there. Of this generation, then, two sons served in the British Army. Their father, the 10th Earl, had long before gone off to his war, too—the Crimean—campaigning in Turkey and Sardinia as a captain, 9th Regiment. The tendency to leave Galway and the family's final removal to England may relate as well to the sons' marrying there; two years before he was killed, William wed a London girl. Gilbert's wife came from Liverpool.

All this happened half a century and more ago. When Martyn was gone, who would remember? Pallas looked already an archaeological site, its past banked up in layers. We walked around the mansion's foundation; in the pasture still stood a few great oak and yew trees. When Dalton's party got out of their carriage here on July 16, 1908, this pasture had been a lawn. In Dalton's photograph, the house resembles the Great Southern Hotel, a massive neoclassic box behind its Doric portico, monumental and hard to imagine at all in these fields. Its virtue must have seemed its solidity, yet it had been struck like a tent. In the picture, it looked as far off as the beehive tombs of Mycenaean Greece, and harder to know.

What had they been thinking to put it here?

Even back in their prime years, the mid-19th century, according to Woodham-Smith, "The fact was that a large number of Irish landlords were hopelessly insolvent. The extravagance of their predecessors, the building of over-large mansions, reckless expenditure on horses, hounds and conviviality, followed by equally reckless borrowing, had brought very many landowners to a point where, however desperate the needs of their tenantry, they were powerless to give any help." And the gentry still in the money rarely stayed home. "Rents were being spent in England or on the Continent; in 1842 it was estimated that £6,000,000 of rents were being remitted out of Ireland, and Kohl, the German traveller, commented on the mansions of absentee landlords, standing 'stately, silent, empty.'"

Besides supporting the social season in London, the cottagers on the land sometimes supported extraordinary careers. Coming to Ireland back in 1588, Richard Boyle, later Earl of Cork, bought up Sir Walter Raleigh's estates as well as "fortie Ploughlands . . . for fortie pounds." His son Robert was born at Lismore Castle in 1627. "He was nursed," says Aubrey in *Brief Lives*, "by an Irish Nurse, after the Irish manner, wher they putt the child into a pendulous Satchell (instead of a Cradle) with a slitt for the Child's head to peepe out. . . . When a boy at Eaton was verie sickly and pale." Although Robert was the Earl's fourteenth son, his father left him a "Rentall" of "3000 pounds per annum: the greatest part is in Ireland." This served to launch him in physics at Leyden and Oxford; he picked up along the way a reading knowledge of Latin, Greek, Hebrew, Chaldean, and Syriac. By 1660 he discovered the rule of gases that we call Boyle's Law and the idea that all substances are made of elements. "Salt, Sulphur and Mercury" were claimed before "to be the true principles of things."

Not many aristocrats so shook the gates of the future or found their "greatest delight is Chymistrey." Here is Elizabeth Bowen, describing some later patrons of that Hotel Plaza of Dublin in *The Shelbourne Hotel*: "The vigorous sons and daughters of absentees found London, and the English *beau monde* in general, to be at the same time costly and unrewarding, and began to feel the pull of their own land. To retrench without ceasing to cut a dash was now the object; money went a long way farther at home. Home therefore, from over the sea, they trooped. There *was* something warming about this compact, miniature Irish social world, with its long-known names, close-woven gossip, its familiar faces. Times might be bad for the landowner—oh, indeed they were!—but somehow one footed the bill for Dublin gaiety."

Martyn now seemed custodian not of all this but of its memory here. In fact, he cared more for the house than for the castle. It was Pallas Castle they came to see—except in my case. He knew we both had to do with the house, with transferring it in some way, I suppose, from him to me. Yet he couldn't do that, he could only stammer a few recollections. Among them happened to be the ones I came after—a stroke of luck. For the rest I could only put down what he and a few others said—the attitudes of some who had known the landed Irish peers from their childhoods or from their lifework. Bowen might write of the Troubles, as she had, "Many of those big, lonely, treed-about country houses, from which, generation after generation, the owners had set out on their trips to Dublin, now became blackened shells with wind whistling through them." But this fate was longer in coming to Pallas. Anthony Nugent held the fort there even after the Free State was set up in 1921 and his seat in the Lords was swept away. From then, Westmeath had scant call for his ermine cape and dress sword; still he held on. With his passing, Pallas was finally surrendered to the twin blows of death duties and worldwide depression.

Before then Flower Hill, too, had slipped from the Nugents, though the wrecker didn't get it. Instead, it had the good fortune to pass into the hands of a Galway family named Walsh. When Martyn and I said goodbye, I set out to call there, asking directions on the way.

The estate lies in Tynagh toward Killimor, about four miles from Pallas. My first guide was a tall girl parked at her house in an English Ford and probably just come from Mass. I drew up window-to-window while she explained the turns to Flower Hill. After that, there was a gatehouse just opposite the drive—a long one leading up to the mansion. She laughed and carefully repeated herself, like sending a child to the store! She'd been right to do this; farther on, I had to stop and ask again. This time it was a rawboned man camping by the road in the mist with his family. He stuck his face in the window.

"Can ye spare a little something? A bit of silver?"

He was desperate.

They were wrapped in dirty rugs, man, wife, and baby. Was their shelter the *scalpeen* of an evicted tenant? No, a tent pitched near a wagon, and by it stood the smallest, most busted donkey I've ever seen. A little fire was going, and they'd made a mess around it on the bank. Behind the red face in the window the woman watched for sentence to be passed.

"Flower Hill? Can you tell me where?"

"Here you are, sir, Flower Hill!"

Sure enough, an empty cottage stood just up the road with gateposts opposite. I gave him a coin that was seven-sided, not round, because that one was worth a dollar. He backed off and I turned into the drive.

The mansion stood on top of a long rise, slate-roofed, huge, of gray stone and surrounded by outbuildings of the same gray stone. One of them had a hole torn in its wall and some balusters on the terrace had crumbled. The place looked like an Italian villa in a war movie, as if shells had exploded and Sophia Loren was coming out. Behind it the hill fell away in a great sweep of valley. Livestock grazed down there, beef cattle and sheep.

A girl, John Walsh's daughter, let me in and took my name to her father. He appeared, a slight, dark man with an easy manner. We went into a little study warmed by an electric heater. The house, like Walsh, seemed unfancy and nice. It was a grab bag filled with the assortment typical of an Irish home, and probably an American one—things handed down, long used, never used, bought on impulse, broken and about to be fixed, broken and never to be fixed. If there was any formal period furniture I didn't see it. Walsh himself looked to be a gentleman farmer, but one who could tend a sick animal as well as handle a column of figures.

I told him the story's short version and he looked at the picture. Had he another chair or two like that in the cellar?

No, never saw it before. And by now it looked as if only five had come to Galway. Walsh sat amused and mildly curious. Like others I took the story to in Ireland, he cared little about the chairs' Philadelphia provenance—that was like asking an American to revere Daniel O'Connell's spittoon! Walsh spoke instead of the time his father purchased Flower Hill from the Nugents. He remembered Gilbert, the 12th Earl, and just barely a little of the finale at Pallas. The 11th Earl on the last round of improvements spent £22,000 and added more than two rooms. And when they pulled the mansion down, they spread its rubble on the lane to surface it. So the stones went from castle to house to road.

"Who are the folks camped by your gate, gypsies?"

"No, no. The gypsies are rich now!"

"Who are they then?"

"Travelers."

"They're Irish? What do they do?"

"Yes, Irish. Travelers. This one doesn't do anything. He will stay for a bit, then go."

Driving toward Loughrea, I kept to the back road. Just before Tynagh village a man hiked along headed that way at a good pace. He was a big lanky fellow in rough clothes and never turned as I passed—the traveler.

My foxhunt in Galway seemed ended.

Now we had documentary evidence of the sale at Pallas of "Five dining room chairs," as well as eyewitness statements by Francis Martyn and his wife that the Fanshawes or their facsimiles once stood there. From the solicitor came the ledger suggesting by omission that these five were acquired after November 1913. Three papers, *The Times, Independent,* and *Connacht Tribune*, probably running the same telephoned account from Loughrea, gave the price as £19. The banquet chairs brought less than $20 each, yet the correspondent thought the bidding "keen." And although Father O'Loughlin's vote of thanks to Messrs. Battersby passed by acclamation, apparently some sleepers of the century had just slipped out the door.

An astonishing thing is that five years before—in April 1929—at the New York sale of the Howard Reifsnyder Collection, the Randolph Sample wing chair made $33,000, and two of the sample side chairs $15,000 and $9,500. However the effect of the depression may be judged, in 1929 the Fanshawe set was worth $50,000 or more. It was hard to escape the conclusion that nobody at Pallas knew what was being sold. Mrs. Connell never imagined what she carried away; her *chattels* slept on until Bourne and De Silva blew the whistle forty years later.

The Fiat from Avis passed a mound by the road, and on impulse I pulled over, then walked back. About a dozen wasted stones stuck in the mound waist-high, making a ring possibly 50 feet across. A cairn of rocks lay piled in its center. At first I had only the foggiest idea of what was here. But these stones didn't belong in a Westmeath portrait and nobody tumbled them out of a Norman fortress either. They belonged instead to the gods, ghouls, and fairies of pagan Ireland. The mound wasn't a dolmen of pillars set up to carry roof stones, but a stone circle. Once had these rocks been idols?

In Galway City later, looking through a book called *Ireland in Pre-Celtic Times* by R. A. S. Macalister, I came across a poem he translated from the Irish which seemed to go with the stone circle. It is the *Dindsheanchus* of Magh Sleacht, maybe 1,000 years old, and it tells of a place like this one with idols surrounding a god named Crom Cruaich:

Stone idols old
Ranked round Cromm Cruaich, four times three,
They were of stone, but he of gold,
The hosts deceiving bitterly.

From Eremon
The gracious founder of our race.
Till Patrick came, they served a stone,
And worshipped it within that place.

With heavy maul
He smashed the paltry gods each one,
With valorous blows destroyed them all,
Nor left a fragment 'neath the sun.

Crom Cruaich is said to have been a center stone decked with gold and silver at Cavan. Rituals at some circles went on into the Christian era.

The idols near Pallas may have been smashed not by Patrick, but by the military monks. If I'm lucky enough ever to see Francis Martyn again, I can ask him.

3
Philadelphians

> Not heaven itself upon the past has pow'r;
> But what has been, has been, and I have had my hour.
> —Dryden

AS THE EVE OF THE AMERICAN Bicentennial approached, Philadelphia seemed to be trying to pull herself together like an old whore. But nothing had changed. When I lived there, Frank Rizzo was police commissioner; now he was mayor. They hadn't even done anything about Broad Street. The taxi bumped into the inner city past the canopies of Italian mortuaries, the skin flicks, and fast food stands. The young blacks who five years before stood waiting on the street corners looked to be still waiting there. Rizzo had had the good sense to put some of them on his police force. Instead of plantings down Broad Street's center island, this Champs Élysées bore hundreds of parked cars and vans jammed bumper-to-bumper under the fall of soot. We passed the old Free Library, boarded up long ago, an abandoned Parthenon recalling now not so much the Greek idea as the strains of *Onward Christian Soldiers* and the 19th-century enterprise of the Biddles, Whartons, Girards, Wanamakers, and Cadwaladers. What led their industry to fail? Who had foreseen the tidal wave of trash, plastic, and flotsam now washing up Broad about their citadel? Parthenon, indeed! *How had we managed to goof so?*

The cab driver, herself an urban black possibly a couple of generations liberated from a plantation on the Delmarva Peninsula, didn't know where the Warwick Hotel was and guessed wrong turning east into Locust Street. She gave me a booklet called *TaxiGab* and told me to look it up.

You don't need a reservation to check into a Philadelphia hotel, and I doubt if you'll be needing one anytime soon. At the Warwick desk I asked for a single. When we came off the elevator, the bellman put the bag down in a large and nicely appointed room with twin beds and bath.

"Is this a single?" "When there's one in here, it's a single. When there's two, it's a double," he explained.

Yet you don't look down over the rooftops from a hotel room or the Whitman Bridge without a sense of wonder at this town, of wonder and outrage. It was probably always like this. Did the model town ever exist? The other day I happened across reflections of a lady visitor to Independence Hall back in 1865, reported then in *Arthur's Home Magazine*:

> The neglected appearance of this time-honored building [the old State House] hallowed in the memory of every American citizen by the most sacred association, is discreditable to Philadelphia; and it is a disgrace to her authorities that, for a paltry rent, the very vestibule of this Temple of Liberty is desecrated by an eating-stand, where coffee and sausages, muffins and pies, cheesecakes and apples are sold to the passing crowds. The fumes of a cook shop load the air and float away up into the steeple.... It is a thing to be wondered at, how Philadelphias can, year after year, tolerate this shameful neglect and improper use of a building which they hold in patriotic trust for the nation. Everything about it is common and mean. It is not even kept in decent repair. The Chestnut street front entrance and windows would shame a liberal gentleman's barns and outbuildings. At the cry of 'shame!' let this shocking desecration cease.

The Historical Society of Pennsylvania fills and will soon overflow a brick building down Locust Street from the hotels about Rittenhouse Square. My walk there was toward the Delaware, the most blah of rivers. The city started on its bank and spread westward. Society Hill, the "good" old neighborhood, occupies a section of the streets numbered Second through Eighth from the river. The doors are topped by fanlights and flanked by Doric columns much as Dublin's, but here the array of brass house number, knocker, and letter slot is apt to be incomplete, the entrance often being supplied instead with a bootscraper. When we started out in the antiques business some years ago, I managed to carry off one of these glorious iron scrapers, like any Goth sacking Rome. Its posts were set with lead in a marble block, so it weighed plenty, and the Pine Street dealer who entrusted this trophy to us had to pay a passer-by to help lift it into the Volkswagen! Only a few of the finer Georgian mansions have escaped us. Before Frances Wister and the Preservation of Landmarks Society came forward in 1931 to save the Powel House, its carved interiors were carted off to the Metropolitan and

Pennsylvania Museums (including a fireplace surround probably by one of Randolph's carvers, Hercules Courtenay). Lately the Powel rooms had held a mattress factory and hair dealer. As early as 1820 the Cadwalader house went down, interiors and all, demolished by its last owner, Stephen Girard.

It happened that although their Second Street home had vanished, the Cadwaladers cared to save their bills and receipts. Apparently they passed from the General's secretary William Gouge and his second wife Williamina Bond Cadwalader to his executor Lambert, then on to the next generations. One of the later executors was a Cadwalader in-law. He recently turned the whole trove over to the Historical Society. The family earlier had sent over reams of 19th-century items—letters, army commissions, commendations for gallantry in the Civil War, and penciled complaints from one of those honored (Dr. Charles) that his citation should have embraced considerably more than only Gettysburg and the "campaign from the Rapidan to the James in 1864." The collection adds up now to about 65,000 pieces of paper. Enough date from before the Revolution so that Nicholas Wainwright has been able to reconstruct the Second Street household on paper with greater precision than that of any other colonial dwelling in Philadelphia, standing or not.

Upstairs in the Historical Society I asked Peter Parker, who runs the Manuscript Department, for all Randolph and Affleck bills and receipts. It wasn't quite that easy. The age of electronic information retrieval hadn't yet arrived. What came down from the stacks in a few minutes were a dozen boxes of sorted and unsorted papers, letters, and scraps, dated and undated, signed and unsigned, readable and illegible—here was the first installment. One piece picked at random like a leaf from a mulch pile seemed to be an account of hay and grain laid by at the General's farm in Maryland. The ink had gone light brown and the paper crumbly as a dead leaf. From London early in 1769 came a letter from Colonel Lloyd's son congratulating Cadwalader on his marriage to Betsy. What rhetoricians they were! At last, thank God, the men of few words—the masons, carpenters, upholders, and other tradesmen—half the day to cull a hundred of these from the cousins' invitations to visit, the state of the tobacco crop at Wye, the health of kin near and far—all their lives collapsed in these cardboard caskets. After two days at the boxes, I pulled exactly five cabinetmakers' bills in any way bearing, even by indirection, on Randolph or the chairs:

May 15, 1770: *"John Cadwalader in Acct with Lambert Cadwalader— . . . to Cash pd Randolph, Joyner £30—"* paid in Pennsylvania money. This compensated Randolph for some work on the house rather than furniture, for another scrap acknowledges receipt of £30 signed in a crabbed hand *Benjamin Randolph—"for Work on his House & Materials."*

November 24, 1770: Randolph billed Cadwalader £252.16.1 for *"Carved Work done at his new House."*

August 27, 1770: William Savery billed for £61.19 worth of furniture—including 19 walnut chairs, no mahogany.

October 13, 1770: Thomas Affleck billed £114.3 for mahogany and other furniture, but no side chairs. *"To Mr Reynold's Bill for Carving the Above £37"* and *"To Barnard & Jugies Ditto for Ditto £24.4."*

July 19, 1771: Francis Trumble billed £9 for 12 *"round top Windsor Chairs @ 15/—"*

Wainwright has found another bill from Randolph dated September 26,1769, for making a bed and window cornices with iron rods and hooks, as well as the entry in Cadwalader's waste (i.e., account) book, October 10, 1769: *"B. Randolph acct for Furniture £94.15."* With this is noted *"2 marble Slabs etc had of C. Coxe, £30."* These, Wainwright finds, came from the Coxe house on Second Street whose contents were auctioned the previous May. If the table frames were included they may now have been discarded and new ones made in Randolph's shop. Two pier tables are called *"marble slabs"* in the April 1786 inventory. At that time the General's widow returned from Shrewsbury to find cracked "one of the marble side-boards." In 1904 Curran got the other one. This Curran (now Metropolitan Museum) table bears a striking resemblance to the first sample chair.

To me the most interesting item in all this was Randolph's furniture credit, for its entry in October 1769 predated by nearly a year Peale's portrait of Lambert. The Cadwaladers then not only had Randolph pieces in hand long before the house was ready; the portrait itself was painted in the summer of 1770 before the parlors were done and probably before the family moved in. The transaction under *"Household Furniture"* passed from John to Lambert, who applied £94.15 to Randolph's furniture account and bracketed with it £30 for *"2 marble slabs etc had of C. Coxe."*

Mr John Cadwalader

1770 To Plunket Fleeson Dr

Octobr 18th To covering over Tail finish'd in Canvis 32 Chairs @ 8/6 — 13 : 13 : 0

— To Sundries for a large Sopha Viz: 15 yds gerth @ 1/ — 3 yds drilla 2/8
13 yds Canvis 16/3 — 23 lb Curled hair @ 1/10 - tacks & thread 1/
11 yds lace @ 1/ — finishing in Canvis & making a Case 35/ — 5 : 9 : 10

To 30 lb wooll @ 1/3 — & making a Mattress 7/6 of Ozna — 2 : 5 : 0

26 To an other Do — 2 : 5 : 0

To a large bed bottom & cord 20/ 1 lesser do 18/ — 1 : 18 : 0

Novr 3 To 2 Cloak pins @ 1/ — 12 do @ 1/6 — 12 hook Do @ 9 —
to Mrs Jones — 1 : 9 : 0

21st To altering Vallts & Cornices of the Check bed (altering) window Curts
putting up & fixing do, & 2 window Curts in the small
back parlour, rods, hooks pins tape tacks &c — 1 : 18 : 0

To making a dark Chince bed — 1 : 10 : 0

6½ yds linin for lining 15/9 — 20 yds white lace 8d 6 yds thread 3/6
bed rods rings tape tacks & silk 25/10 — 2 : 13 : 5

Decemr 5th To 30 lb wooll & making an Ozna Mattress — 2 : 5 : 10

15 To a pr large single Branches — 2 : 5 : 0

To 22 yds brown ticks @ 2/3 49/6 making 2 beds & bolsters 10/ 2 : 19 : 6

To 3 short post bedsteads & bottoms — @ 43/ — 6 : 9 : 0

26th To 56 yds fine red & white Copper plate Cotton — @ 7/ — 19 : 12 : 0
making of Do a fleetron bed full trim'd, with Plumes, bases,
& head board, fringes, — 3 : 10 : 0
making 2 Win. Curts Do — @ 12/6 — 1 : 5 : 0
16 yds linin for lining Valls &c @ 2/8 6 yds coarse do @ 2/ — 2 : 13 : 8
118 yds fringe for bed & window Curtns — @ 2/ — 11 : 16 : 0
— 19 Large Tassels @ 2/ — 38 small Do — @ 1/6 — 5 : 8 : 0
25 yds Silk lace @ 8d — 32 yds white twill'd lace @ 1/ — 1 : 7 : 4
1 yd wide Muslin 8/ thread tape, rings, tacks, tenter hooks &c 14/8 — 1 : 2 : 8
38 yds line @ 5d 15/10 — bed rods, hooks & pins, 26/ — 2 : 1 : 10

To 33 lb wooll & making an Ozna Mattress — 2 : 8 : 9

To fixing & putting up the new Chince bed, Cloak pins, tacks 0 : 12 : 6

Carried over — £98 : 18 : 4

Received 1 August 1771 of Mr John Cadwalader the Sum of One
Hundred & Sixty three Pounds Eighteen Shill 9d & 3½ in full

Plun: Fleeson

Bill from Plunket Fleeson to John Cadwalader, 1771
—Historical Society of Pennsylvania

One of many upholstering jobs done by Plunket Fleeson was: October 18, 1770: *"To covering over Rail finish'd in Canvis 32 Chairs @ 8/6—£13.13.0."* Here the words *"covering over Rail"* are interesting. The second sample and Fanshawes are stuffed and partially covered over the seat rails—unusual in American Chippendale side chairs. Most have "slip seats" made of framed pads that fit in the rails. For example, of twenty-one Philadelphia Chippendale side chairs pictured by Albert Sack in his *Fine Points of Furniture,* only one is upholstered over the rails. (The Fanshawes' rails look un-American, too — these cyma curves come from the gilt salons of Europe, pure Louis XV.) Words new or old can fool us, but what Fleeson implies here is that by the autumn of 1770 Cadwalader had at least 32 chairs upholstered in the general style of the Fanshawes.

How much furniture did £94.15 buy?

A good deal. William Savery's bill itemized side chairs: *"To 6 Walnut lether Bottom Chairs | @ 26S—7.16.10"* and *"To 12 Walnut Chairs Stuff'd & Canvas'd @ 24S—14.8.0."* A chair of this sort, then, cost a little over £1. Affleck's bill is revealing, too. He charges £5 apiece *"To 2 Commode Card Tables,"* £10 *"To a Mahogany desk,"* and £4.10 *"To an Easy Chair."* The carvers' charges raise the cost by half, but even so these pieces look like astonishing bargains, especially as Savery and Affleck both turned out superlative furniture.

What about the two card tables? On sighting Affleck's bill it seemed that one table might survive at Winterthur, also pictured by Joseph Downs in his *American Furniture.* Downs pedigrees it as "Ex. coll. Cadwalader." The top and frame are rectilinear and don't resemble the serpentine table in the General's family portrait, but the legs and hairy-paw feet certainly do. Downs connects this Du Pont table to the Cadwaladers with the circumstance that it and a pier glass came from a dealer who got them from a member of the famiy in 1949. Both pieces, now in the Blackwell parlor at Winterthur along with the second sample chair, were inherited in 1875 by Dr. Charles's sister, Mrs. Henry J. Rowland (Anne Cadwalader). Until 1889 she left her pier glass hanging in the back bedroom of the mansion at 240 South Fourth Street.

At any rate the picture emerging isn't of one master plugging away at the prize chairs, but of furniture being carted unfinished, or "in the white," to the carvers James Reynolds, Bernard & Jugiez, Hercules Courtenay, Pollard & Butts, or others. Such subcontracting was a general thing. In attributing the Fanshawes to Benjamin Randolph

Philad^a Octr 13th 1770

Mr John Cadwalader

To Thos. Affleck Dr.

Date	Item	£
Octr 13	To a Mahogany desk	10.–.–
	To a Bedstead w^t Casters Brass Cap^s &c Compleat	12.–.–
	To altering another Bedstead	2.–.–
	To Repairing and Cleaning Sundry Furniture	1.10.–
Novr 7	To polishing & oiling 5 mahogany doors @ 5/	1.5.–
Decr 20	To a Sett of Cutt open Cornices Rails & pulleys	2.–.–
	To 2 Window ditto @ 10/	1.–.–
	To 2 Mahogany Commode Sopheas for the Recesses @ £8	16.–.–
	To one Large ditto	10.–.–
	To an Easy Chair to Sute ditto	4.10.–
1771 Jany 2	To 2 Commode Card Tables @ £5	10.–.–
4	To 2 mahogany knife Trays @ 14/	1.8.–
11	To a mahogany Tea Table	4.10.–
	To a mahogany Breakfast Table	3.10.–
14	To a ditto Night Table Compleat	5.–.–
	To 4 Mahogany fire screens @ 2.10	10.–.–
	To a Mahogany desk	11.–.–
	To one horse fire Screen w^t 3 leaves	4.–.0
	To a Mahogany harpsicord Frame	4.10.–
		£114.3.–

To Mr Reynold's Bill for Carving the Above £37
To Barnard & Jugies Ditto for Ditto £24.4
£61.4

Item	£
To 8 Blinds @ 20	3.–.–
To 3½ yd^s silk	1.15.–
To Cutting a frame	10.–
	£119.8.–

Bill from Thomas Affleck to John Cadwalader, 1770
—Historical Society of Pennsylvania

what's meant is that he took the order and laid on the design, his joiners and apprentices cut and joined the chairs, and they may or may not have been carved down the street.

Might the Fanshawes instead have been made in the shop of Thomas Affleck?

The short answer has to be maybe.

No chair with Affleck's label in it has been found, and attributions to him are generally based on his association with patrons such as the Penns and the Fishers. This is to say, a side chair descending from Thomas Fisher has always been given to Affleck because he's known to have worked for this Quaker family soon after he reached Philadelphia in 1763. In much the same way, the samples are attributed to Randolph through association with his own family. Nothing about Affleck pieces—if they *are* Affleck pieces—suggests he might have had anything at all to do with an old monster like the sample wing chair. Yet the riddle is that, with its front legs doweled Queen Anne-style into a massive oak frame, this easy chair doesn't look much like Randolph's thing, either.

Infra-red photographs of the Fanshawe seat rails have been taken, and those who've had the chance to study them, including Winterthur's curator, agree that they started out with the second sample chair. *It* descended from Randolph's stepson, Nathaniel Fenimore. The idea that Fenimore got hold of several variant chairs more or less like the super-rococo one on his stepfather's trade card, but made by Affleck, seems pretty farfetched. In those days who'd have bought six different single chairs made by anybody?

When S. W. Woodhouse, Jr., researched the sample chairs, he discovered that five of them had been purchased from Fenimore's decendants and one still was left in the family. Fenimore's mother, Mary Wilkinson Fenimore Randolph, willed on June 1, 1816, after other bequests: "All the remainder of my household goods I give unto my son, Nathaniel Fenimore." Nathaniel's daughter Rebecca, born in 1831, married her cousin Samuel Zelley. From her family soon after 1900 three of the chairs passed to the Philadelphia merchant and collector Howard Reifsnyder and at least one to James Curran. Curran's was the first sample. The second chair is recorded in his family by 1927, owned by Thomas A. Curran, who may have willed or given it to Charles Curran.

Woodhouse's 1927 *Antiques* article adds some interesting details about the first chair:

> Twenty-five years ago "Jimmy" Curran heard rumors, hunted up and bought a fine chair. It was one of six that old wives' tales had frequently referred to as "the six sample chairs." By judicious efforts the entire six were ultimately unearthed, though one still remains in the family of original ownership. . . . The first was bought by the Doyen of American collectors, Henry W. Erving, of Hartford. He found it in Curran's treasury one hot summer's day as he was returning from his son's commencement at Johns Hopkins. Of this chair Luke Vincent Lockwood says, "It is the best chair that has been found in this country." Three others of the six, one wing and two side chairs, are in the collection of Howard Reifsnyder, of Philadelphia.*

If Woodhouse's chronology is accurate, James Curran got the first sample about 1902. He also went into Davis & Harvey's in November 1904, paying the sale's top price, $450, for the marble-top pier table. The legs and scroll feet of this table, purchased by the Metropolitan Museum in 1918, look remarkably like those on the first sample chair. That James Curran left without topping the $180 bid next day on the set of ten mahogany side chairs suggests that the mates to the second sample weren't these. That he of all people would have known their value is confirmed by the fact that when the Currans did get the second sample it was held in the family until finally sold to H. F. Du Pont in 1948. By then Du Pont had succeeded Erving as the dean of Americana collectors; what he put into his homes at Winterthur and on Long Island cost him nearly $70 million.

Inferences, however carefully made, are always slippery, but the dead don't talk. What could we believe?

First, the Fanshawes might be attributed only to the maker of the second sample chair. Its descent from his widow certainly pointed to Randolph. The trail of the samples via the Zelleys was more than an old wives' tale; besides Woodhouse's work, Marion D. Iverson has succeeded in finding a member of that family who told her the tradition is true. †

Second, a curious design detail of the marble-top pier table appears also in three of the sample chairs, all the Fanshawes, and the serpentine card table. This is the small cabochon—literally, a convex gem stone—carved by the joint of each front leg and skirt (see illustration, Appendix 4). This little kidney makes the very kernel of the rococo style, but we

*Since 1927 all the samples have changed hands. The present museum owners of four are given in the picture captions, while two are now unlocated.

† Telephone conversation with writer, October 1976.

First sample chair
—ex-Coll. Henry W. Erving,
Hartford, Conn.

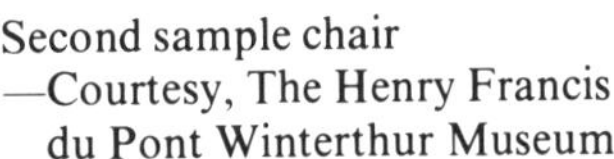

Second sample chair
—Courtesy, The Henry Francis
du Pont Winterthur Museum

Third sample chair
—Colonial Williamsburg

Fourth sample chair
—Philadelphia Museum of Art:
Harrison Fund Income

Fifth sample chair (wing chair)
—Philadelphia Museum of Art:
Purchased: Museum Fund

Sixth sample chair
—Courtesy *The Magazine Antiques*

Now unlocated. The Gothic splat and simple lines depart from the other samples'. Recent reprints of Woodhouse's May 1927 *Antiques* article put this chair in the Garvan Collection at Yale University, but it's not there and never has been.

Penciled on shoe, chair VII:
C. Hanlon John Wannamakers Phila

—Courtesy of Israel Sack, Inc., N.Y.C.

Penciled on shoe, chair VIIII:
C. Hanlon J Wannamaker

—Courtesy of Israel Sack, Inc., N.Y.C.

Cadwalader marble-top pier table
—Metropolitan Museum of Art

One of the General's best-documented pieces, this table's top was one of *"2 marble Slabs etc had of C. Coxe, £30"* in 1769. That Randolph's shop made the table frame seems confirmed by the joining of this notation in Cadwalader's waste book with the entry: *"B. Randolph acct for furniture, £94.15."*

can find it at just this place in no other American chairs in the literature. It, among other features, links these hairy-paw pieces to the marble-top table. John Cadwalader's waste book entry of October 10, 1769, may link the marble slab to Randolph. The "kidney" cabochons pop up, too, on the mantelpiece panels in the Blackwell house parlor, and there is cause to believe these panels may have been designed or executed, or both, by Randolph's carver, Hercules Courtenay (Appendix 3).

Finally, the Fanshawes were not likely offered for sale in the 1904 auction, because Curran let all the sets of chairs go cheap.

One of Thomas Jefferson's biographers says that on a spring day in 1776 the carpenter Ben Randolph delivered to his lodger in his house on Chestnut Street a small portable desk of Jefferson's own design. Ben the carpenter marveled at the piece, though made by his own hands. The desk is now in the Library of Congress.

In fact, by 1776 Randolph was no more a carpenter than Chippendale. He was an entrepreneur of nerve, taste, and connections, and a master joiner who perhaps led in introducing the rococo fashion to America. His custom seems to have been rivaled in Philadelphia only by Savery, Affleck, and, later, Gostelowe. These names have been slow to emerge from the other-directed Victorian century, and only about fifty years ago, working in and out of the then Pennsylvania Museum, did Samuel Woodhouse, Jr., pick up Randolph's trail. To Woodhouse and Marian Day Iverson, whose book *The American Chair* culls some more early material, we mainly owe this account of Randolph's life and doings.* His receipt book for 1763–77 is at Winterthur.

The family name he left behind in New Jersey was Fitz-Randolph. His birthdate is reported by Iverson to be January 30, 1737/38. Randolph first appears in Philadelphia with his wedding February 18, 1762, to Anna Bromwich, a stay maker's daughter. When Anna's father died the next year, the Bromwich house on Sassafras Street passed to her. Now Randolph termed himself a "joiner." He lived in 1765–66 on Arch Street. The following year Thomas Shoemaker sold Randolph his shop on Chestnut Street. This one was succeeded, or possibly augmented, by

* A source for their researches as well as ours has been Alfred Coxe Prime, *The Arts and Crafts in Philadelphia, Maryland and South Carolina* (The Walpole Society, 1929). Prime was an engineer for the Pennsylvania Railroad who with his wife's help collected and classified about 20,000 tradesmen's ads from early newspapers. Woodhouse wrote the introduction and Prime's two volumes were published posthumously in an edition of 500 copies.

Randolph's ultimate establishment, a new and bigger house and shop built in 1769 on a Chestnut Street lot rented from James Hamilton. Woodhouse has turned up city tax records in which the joiner progressed to "cabinetmaker" in 1768, then "carver and gilder," then "merchant." Finally, in 1786, he was taxed £176.11, with property at five locations in and near the city, "two horses, cattle and one Negro." But by this time Randolph must have lived part of the year at his country place in Burlington, New Jersey. He now called himself a "gentleman." Nearby stood the family sawmill, Speedwell Works, owned until 1778 by his brother Daniel.

The Library Company of Philadelphia has one of his rather lush trade cards, engraved in 1770 by James Smither and garnished with furniture and decorative tidbits lifted from various London style books. Randolph was now set up "*at the Golden Eagle in Chesnut Street Between third and fourth Streets,*" where he turned out "*all Sorts of Cabinet & Chairwork Likewise Carving, Gilding &c Perform'd in the Chinese and Modern Tastes.*" Here Modern equates with fashionable and French rococo. The tall case clock to our right on the trade card has been traced to Thomas Johnson's *Designs for Furniture* (London, 1758). The bearded bust atop the ware room seems to have been copied from Plate 108 of Chippendale's 1762 *Director*. The side chair on our left looks something like the second sample but still more like the "*Ribband Back*" ones shown in all editions of Chippendale's guide. The secretary at the bottom comes from Plate 108, too. Next to it on the card somebody seems to have left his fingerprint. And scattered about in embryonic form are the kidney cabochons.

The fuss over the workability of Chippendale's etherealized pieces upset their author, who in his 1762 preface got around to his critics: "I shall repay their Censures with Contempt. Let them unmolested deal out their pointless Abuse, and convince the World they have neither Good-nature to commend, Judgment to correct, nor Skill to execute what they find Fault with."

Some of the *Abuse* seems to have come not from the idea that Chippendale didn't know how to make fine furniture, but the fact that his designers didn't always know how to draw it.

A curious thing about the American Revolution is that it got borne forward by so many men of means and accomplishment with a good deal to lose.

Randolph's shop turned by lathe wooden buttons to discourage

Benjamin Randolph's trade card
—Library Company
of Philadelphia

importing metal ones, and in the *Pennsylvania Journal* on March 15, 1770, he found it unnecessary "to say anything in their praise, or by way of recommendation of them, as he doubts not but every lover of his country will encourage the same, as well as all other American manufactures, especially at this time, when the importation of British superfluities is deemed inconsistent with the true interest of America." In 1774 Randolph joined about two dozen others to establish the First City Troop, supplying his own horse, uniform, and side arms. The troop crossed to Trenton with Washington, perhaps serving as dispatch riders and guarding prisoners. Some were detailed after Princeton as Washington's bodyguards. But like Cadwalader's, Randolph's service in the field proved intermittent; probably Washington could neither mess nor employ such a galaxy of knights. Before May 6, 1777, Randolph was back home, for on that date he ran an ad in the Pennsylvania *Evening Post:*

> *Holsters, pistols, carbines, swords for the Light Horse wanted immediately. Inquire of Benjamin Randolph in Chestnut Street.*

That spring Martha Washington traveled from Virginia to join her husband at his headquarters in Morristown, and on her way she stayed in Randolph's new house by the Sign of the Golden Eagle. The General noted to one of his staff on May 3: "Mrs. Washington . . . begs that you enquire what she has to pay at Mr. Randolph's (in Chestnut Street) for the night or two she was there on her way up, and pay it." Apparently that month Randolph shuttled back and forth, since a letter dated May 11, 1777, from Washington to Congress was sent "by Mr. Randolph of Chestnut Street."

For a time we didn't know how Randolph's fortunes fared during the British occupation of Philadelphia, but soon he quit business.* In November 1778, a few months after the British troops departed, he advertised "*A Quantity of Carvers and Cabinet-Makers Tools . . . for sale at public vendue*" together with furniture and some mahogany. By 1781 he was buying property next to Benjamin Franklin's lot and selling a parcel of his late wife's inheritance. His daughters Mary and Anna, not yet adult, are named in this last deed as "Heiresses at Law" to their mother's property.

*A lately discovered and surprising cause of Randolph's closing his shop is given in Chapter 5.

Randolph is glimpsed twice more in the public record in 1782, advertising property for sale with the explanation, "*intending to leave the state.*" But apparently his return to New Jersey turned out temporary or seasonal; at any rate, he owned considerable property in Philadelphia as late as 1786. After the war he married Mary Wilkinson Fenimore, widowed like himself. The bride had at least two children, Nathaniel and Priscilla, to match his two. They lived at least part of the year at Burlington on the New Jersey side of the Delaware River, and in 1790 Randolph went into nearby Trenton to sign his will. The will's provisions don't help us at all!

> Whereas there was a verbal agreement between me and my wife, Mary, previous to marriage, that neither of us would claim any right in any property of the other, in consequence I have not meddled in her real or personal estate, therefore I bequeath to my said wife, Mary £20."

On Randolph's death, only one of his daughters, Anna, still lived, and she then moved to Morristown. As noted earlier, her stepmother made her own will in 1816, bequeathing the bulk of her estate to her son Nathaniel Fenimore. He was charged with giving a home to his sister Priscilla until she married. The Zelleys from whom came the sample chairs were left them later on by Nathaniel's daughter, Rebecca Fenimore Zelley.

Here was the sum and substance of the samples' apparent source as mined from the record by Woodhouse. We must believe that Randolph kept these chairs when he liquidated at the Golden Eagle and that later on Anna Randolph left them with her stepmother.

The pre-nuptial agreement leading Randolph to bequeath his wife only £20 has seemed a problem to some, but actually a widow is rarely stripped of all her household goods. Apparently a situation like this arose on the death in Philadelphia of Samuel Powel's father. A letter from Powel to his uncle on December 26, 1764, suggests that even then the widow's share was protected by law: "*The Furniture was, by Will, equally divided between my Sisters & self. The Widow's Third I purchased, so that two Thirds of it are now my Property.*"

After several days of going through the boxes in the Manuscript Department, I wandered out into the reading room, eyesore and backsore. Something about a public reading room puts people on the defensive, or at least puts me on the defensive. (*Are you queer, or don't*

Carved detail in the Fanshawe chairs. Casters were fitted in feet at some point, then taken off. The occasional larger-than-nail holes along the curves in the rails appear as well in the sample wing chair.
—Courtesy of Israel Sack, Inc., N.Y.C.

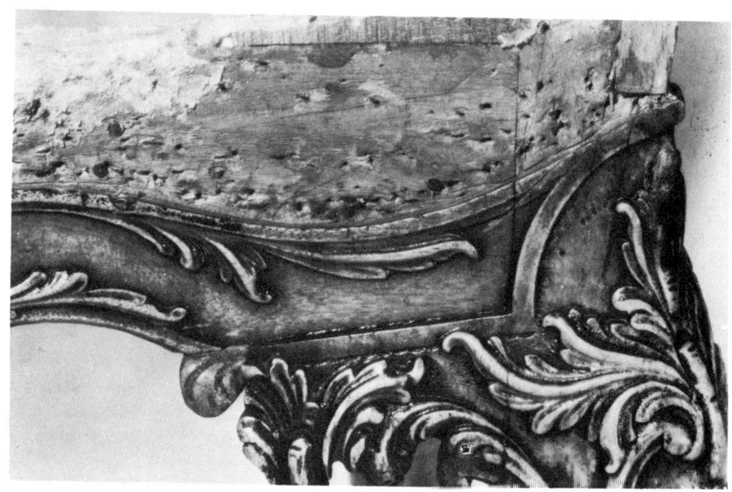

you have anything else to do?) The thing is to demonstrate resolution, however weary of your display the library staff may have grown!

Nearly a whole section of wall was filled with business and other directories, including year after year of Gopsill's *Philadelphia City Directory*. Gopsill's turn-of-the-century volumes must have been financed largely by their block-type ads with pointing hands and neo-Gothic artwork: "JOHN WANAMAKER CITY HALL SQUARE PHILADELPHIA *Wall Papers and Interior Decoration* ALSO NEW YORK CITY B'WAY AT 9TH STREET AND PARIS 44 RUE DES PETITES ECURIES." From the Philadelphia store in 1905 came a scrap of a bill, fallen from the letter file in the other room, charging the Historical Society $5.75 for "Recovering library table in red felt." The store sent a man over to Locust Street to do the work.

I pulled the book for 1899 and ran through the listings for *Hanlon*, but none fitted. The 1900 volume drew a blank too. Then we hit. At least four of the five years following had him:

1901—Hanlon, Chas., upholsterer, 626 S. Bambrey
1902—(volume missing)
1903—Hanlon, Chas., upholsterer, 1913 Brandywine
1904—Hanlon, Chas. M. upholsterer, 1932 Parrish
1905—Hanlon, Chas. M., upholsterer, 1932 Parrish
1906—(not listed)
1907—(volume missing)
1908—(not listed)

Facts, glorious facts, with their gaps, scratches, and bumps! The inscriptions now looked bracketed between 1901 and 1905.

The reading room had turned to a fruitful grove of academe. Every senior citizen pleating his newspaper there was a searcher after truth!

After copying the listings I walked across town to Stouffer's and ordered leg of lamb.

Nicholas Biddle Wainwright has both Biddle and Cadwalader ancestors. He started work at the Historical Society of Pennsylvania in 1939 and was still there. Having served as Director, he was now Director Emeritus. By now his published work ranks him among the top living historians of Pennsylvania. One reason he proved hard to find is that museum people have learned to hide, and the other is that I was mistakenly looking for an old man. They told me he was in the building. At last I went along the top floor knocking at each room until one occupant, a tall man with a black moustache, said he was Wainwright.

He motioned for me to sit. After telling him what a help his book had been, I ventured the Fanshawe chairs would be in it had he published ten years later.

"Nobody knows what chairs were in that house," Wainwright said.

He opened in a pleasant tone, but it poured like ice water. This wasn't really what I'd come to hear. For a few minutes I rehearsed De Silva's and Sack's parts, and the penciled inscriptions.

He said, "They were broken up?"

"One to the Metropolitan, one to Williamsburg, and the others to collectors."

Wainwright leaned back behind the desk in his shirtsleeves and recalled the day he'd gone with Du Pont to examine the Cadwalader portraits and card table:

"Harry Du Pont got down on his hands and knees to look at the feet."

At length he relented a bit on the Fanshawe chairs. Had I considered the possibility that they were taken abroad by the second Mrs. John Cadwalader or her daughter?

As he'd written, the General and his second wife, a Philadelphia beauty born Williamina Bond, had two children, Thomas and Frances, who lived to adulthood. In 1799 Frances married David Montague Erskine (the 2nd Lord Erskine), who later served as British Minister to the United States. Settling eventually in England, the Erskines had 12 children and some financial ups and downs, especially the latter. After it became clear that her son-in-law had inherited little besides a title and unthrifty ways, Mrs. Cadwalader found herself loath to trust him with any money. However, she sailed over to pay the Erskines a visit and, getting on the way a horror of seasickness, stayed for thirty years—the rest of her life. In 1837 she was buried in Crawley, Sussex.

Actually, the prospect that Mrs. Cadwalader or Frances Erskine shipped the chairs to England knocked on the lid of a Pandora's box full of possibilities, all hopeless of proof. Much of the General's furniture was left to his son Thomas, who from 1814 lived in a house at Ninth and Arch in Philadelphia. However, the General's three daughters by his first wife Betsy also inherited goods after Williamina died, and Williamina's daughter inherited, as well. Among them they scattered their legacies of art, silver, furniture, and money from New York and Maryland to Britain. One example is rather interesting. Maria, the little girl who sat on the knee of her young nurse Anne Dingwell, grew up to become Mrs. Samuel Ringgold, living the rest of her years on a prosperous Maryland estate called Fountain Park. (It was on the Ringgolds that Mrs. Sarah Dingwell Peny and her husband came calling one day from Pittsburgh. Maria declined to see her.) After Maria died in 1811, Samuel Ringgold found himself broke and liquidated the property. About a century and a half later, in 1964, an American gallery offered for sale from Fountain Park a portrait of Maria by Gilbert Stuart. The dealer got it not in Maryland but from a descendant of the Ringgolds in England.

These doings in the cadet branches of the family should have scuttled me right here except for one thing, and this was Charles Hanlon's habit of doodling on his work. Hanlon did his bit on the chairs not in England, New York, or Maryland, but in Philadelphia. So in connection with Mrs. Cadwalader and the Erskines I said, "Wanamaker & Company wasn't in business at all until around 1870."

Wainwright nodded.

"Have you ever seen a photograph of Bridget Mary?" I asked.

"No, never."

"I'll bet she was one neat looking girl."

"With a nicely turned pair of ankles!"

Nobody knows what chairs were in that house.

There's no *A for Effort* in pursuing an error. Had Wainwright with one amiable remark pushed me back to square one? Now I had to toss in bed at the Warwick, contemplating each piece of evidence connecting the Fanshawes to John Cadwalader. There were at least four—the two paintings by Peale, the card table, and the "marble slab." Like Sack, I'd seen enough of photographs.

In the morning I phoned Captain John Cadwalader. He retired from active duty in the U.S. Navy a few years ago after serving afloat and ashore, including one tour in Antarctica. In World War II on board the carrier *USS Monterey*, he was a shipmate of Gerald Ford's. Counting from the first American John Cadwalader, who came from Wales in 1697, he's the seventh to bear the name. The Peale portraits as well as the prize card table are now his.

I explained the cause of my visit and Cadwalader agreed I might come out a couple of days later for a look. Neither the paintings nor the table are kept in his home and, allowing the hazard of theft, he asked that I not write about where they are kept. In the spring they'd be going on loan to the Bicentennial show at the Philadelphia Museum. Captain John had heard a little about the Fanshawe chair sale. But he never met his great aunt, Mrs. Charles. Once or twice in the Navy he got to England and had wanted to go see her, but never managed it.

"I think she may have taken those five chairs to London," I said.

"I believe she did, too," Cadwalader said.

When we hung up, I called the number he gave me. Two afternoons later at the appointed hour I found myself getting down on my hands and knees under the card table, as Henry of Winterthur had once done.

It's an amazing piece. Its pinched corners gave it an airborne look, a supersonic bird from the past. With a borrowed flashlight I probed the underparts. One leg swings out to bear the top when it is open, and in this position a small drawer slides from the inner skirt. The drawer was turned near black, as unfinished pine may in time. On the spot I couldn't identify either this wood or the glueblocks, but S. W. Woodhouse ("More About Benjamin Randolph," *Antiques*, January 1930) has found the drawer to be of poplar and yellow pine. These are American materials.* He believes this table was fashioned after the second sample chair. I was sorry to see it's been revarnished, however expertly.

Neither the table nor the portraits have ever been owned outside the family, although the latter got lodged in the HSP for a time by the departing Dr. Charles. Captain John's grandfather, the banker John Cadwalader (1843–1925), inherited the card table. He moved from his birthplace at 240 South Fourth Street possibly when he married in 1866, and in 1886 the family house at 1519 Locust Street passed to him. The table went there, but the paintings stayed with his brother Dr. Charles at South Fourth. Someone in the family has told Wainwright that for years nobody knew this was the very card table in Peale's painting—the discovery was announced by an 8-year-old boy, Captain John's brother Henry, about 50 years ago! When Dr. Charles's father died in 1879, the portrait, now one of Peale's most celebrated paintings, was appraised for probate at $2.

And now on the wall just above the table, the General, Betsy, and baby Anne regarded one another. What fine looking people they were! To this idyll of the shared peach from the orchard, Peale came at the

*The Wharton highboy, a high-style Philadelphia piece owned in 1778 by Joseph Wharton of Walnut Grove, also has drawers of poplar and pine. This type of highboy was never made in England.

season to catch them in their bloom. It didn't much outlast the peach. Within four years, Betsy lay in St. Peter's churchyard near her Second Street house; in fourteen years her husband was buried at Shrewsbury Church. Anne Cadwalader Kemble, her patrimony wasted by high living and her husband's business failure, finished her life much later in New York City as a widowed teacher. Here again (for us) looms the specter of scattered chairs. When Mrs. Kemble's belongings are sold up to satisfy creditors in New York in the spring of 1810, she sends a letter to Thomas, her half-brother in Philadelphia: "If you could see my heart it would be sufficient to convince you of the gratitude I feel for your wishing me to keep some of the furniture, but I had rather not keep any." However, in any case she did keep her parlor chairs and sofas. When Anne died forty years later, these pieces may have passed to her daughter in Boston, Mrs. William H. Sumner.

Lambert Cadwalader's portrait on the wall opposite clearly had belonged to a set of which others then hung in the room, too, among them two of Lambert's father and mother. The canvas sizes were all 51″ by 41″. None of these three is signed or dated; John Cadwalader's account book indicates they were painted in the summer of 1770. He paid James Reynolds to carve three identical frames, which he later had Hercules Courtenay copy to frame the 1772 portrait of Betsy, Anne, and himself. A fifth portrait, of his sister Martha, is signed "*C. Peale pinxt 1771*." Courtenay framed that one, too. Wainwright, to whom we owe the documentation of this and much else, believes all five were designed to fill a number of molded wall panels in the Second Street front parlor. The April 1786 inventory lists "*5 family pictures*" in the front parlor.

The artist, although from Maryland, came to know his patron very well. He painted one or more fine pieces of furniture into each portrait. It looks as if Peale had to lift the card table, as well as the chair, off the floor to compose them with his subjects.

In 1770, of course, John Cadwalader was no rebel general, but a 28-year-old arrival into the Philadelphia *haut monde*. His father, Dr. Thomas Cadwalader, was a widely respected physician and co-founder with Franklin of the Library Company of Philadelphia. His mother, born Hannah Lambert, came from a propertied Trenton family. They sent out their two sons endowed with everything except a lot of money, and after John met the Lloyds, he got that. Before John's marriage, the brothers ran a shop selling dry goods. There is then something of the new rich in their figures and behind them, as if in place of all this extravagantly carved mahogany Peale painted them leaning on Cadillacs. When Lambert stood for his portrait, his occupation was to deal with the tradesmen transforming the Second Street house. To believe the chair he leans on was his, we'd need to suppose that the young bachelor lately commissioned the making of fine furniture and that he had his own home to keep it in. What of the elder Cadwaladers? They could afford to have furniture made, but with their family now shrinking, why should they? Another detail argues against their owning this chair—why would John have a card table made to match a chair in his parents' house?

Lambert's portrait, too, looked a handsome one—he stands in a pale blue suit, awaiting his turn of fortune's wheel, ready for war or peace. His lot fell out better than most. As a colonel six years later, he was captured in the feeble defense of upper Manhattan, but the British paroled him out of regard for his father. He came into Greenwood, a country place near Trenton, was elected to Congress, and acted for years as co-executor of his brother's estate. The younger generation coming along gave him plenty to think about.

I held a photo of chair II against the portrait. Peale's chairback accurately repeated the lines and spatial relationships in the photograph. He also simplified, omitting the inverted *fleur de lis* under the crestrail and replacing the carved leaves on the backrail with one brushed line down its center. The colors are brown on black, so the chair doesn't reproduce well. Peale's grandson, Horace Sellers, has said that entries were made in the artist's diary about the pains he took in getting accessories and other details as he saw them. This doesn't mean, we think, that he cared to stand all day attempting a mirror reflection of each prop. The oval glass above the chair is a mere suggestion of one—we can't even see how its frame is decorated. The scene on Lambert's left may be a framed landscape, a decorated window blind, or actual parklike greenery; it's hard to say. Peale simply didn't choose to render any of these things in detail. In the family portrait a good deal of carving is shown, but the C-scroll on the table's skirt has been shortened by half—probably to mask Betsy's thigh, since Peale has obliged her to straddle the table leg. The artist has resorted to another amusing distortion in hanging both pieces of furniture in the air, at least figuratively. The table closed is 29" high. All known chairs of the Fanshawe design are just under 37" high. Had they actually leveled with

Fanshawe Chair XIII
—Colonial Williamsburg

Colonel Lambert Cadwalader by Charles Willson Peale, 1770
—Captain John Cadwalader USN, Ret.

Card table
Probably made by Thomas Affleck in 1770 with carving by James Reynolds or Bernard & Jugiez. One of a pair. Mahogany; the hidden drawer is yellow pine and poplar and the fly-rail white oak. 29″ H x 39½″ L x 15¼″ W (closed)
—Captain John Cadwalader USN, Ret.

John Cadwalader Family by Charles Willson Peale, 1772
—Captain John Cadwalader USN, Ret.

the brothers as painted, John and Lambert couldn't have topped 5 feet!

While Peale was including some Cadwalader treasures, he found room over the chair to brush in an oval looking glass. On December 5, 1770, James Reynolds billed for four looking glasses, two of them oval, in carved and burnished gold frames. The next March he tacked on a whopping £54 *"To 3, ½ Length Picture frames in Burnish Gold."* The leaf on these frames *is* gold. Peale described the family portrait as *"half Length Sise."* Since those of Lambert and his parents were painted in the summer of 1770, the dates on Reynold's bill may seem a difficulty. He notes a prior payment of £30, however, and has to wait until June 29, 1771, to receipt for the balance due.

Accepting this evidence that John Cadwalader paid for the Lambert frame and an entry in his waste book that he paid Peale £110 for the three portraits plus two miniatures, it seems safe that he owned Lambert's portrait. That he kept this portrait is confirmed by the fact that Lambert's son, Thomas McCall Cadwalader, did not inherit it, passing as it has to Captain John down the senior line of descent. These details have needed looking at carefully, since the 1770 portraits could not have been painted conveniently in the unready Second Street house, but were painted *for* the house.

S.W. Woodhouse thinks both the card table and the chair were modeled on the second sample presumably then in Randolph's shop. Here occurred to us the illogic of Cadwalader's ordering either a card table to match one chair or a single chair to match the table. The young couple were then furnishing their first home by plan. They needed, or thought they needed, many side chairs. Actually, the total approached 100. On October 18,1770, the upholsterer Plunket Fleeson, as noted above, billed £13.13 for finishing thirty-two chairs in canvas for the house, and the following January added charges for making *"3 Sopha's & 76 Chair Cases"* in *"fine Saxon blue."*

From the remarkable trove of papers back at the HSP comes a wartime document marked *Inventory of Gen. Cadwalader's Furniture, as left by General Knyphausen, June 16th 1778.*

After winning at the Brandywine and then smashing a thrust by the Americans at Germantown, General Sir William Howe entered Philadelphia behind his troops in October 1777. Howe set himself up in the Second Street house, but finding it too cramped for his retinue moved to a larger one on Market Street. He turned Cadwalader's over to General

Wilhelm von Knyphausen, his Hessian commander. Knyphausen, the victor at Fort Washington, was said to spread butter on his bread with his thumb. Cadwalader took the precaution the year before of having some of his finer things carted to Shrewsbury plantation, and a surviving letter suggests he may have sent more of the furniture to the house of a friend in Lancaster, Jasper Yeates. He need scarcely have bothered! Knyphausen proved a wonderful tenant. On his departure in June 1778, he paid rent to Cadwalader's agent, left the wine in the cellar just as he found it, and asked the agent to check the contents against what looks like a meticulous count of the furniture made on his arrival a few months before. The Knyphausen inventory lists a total of 92 chairs, of which fourteen stood in the servants' quarters. It puts *In the large front parlour—4 tables—two mahagoni & two marble plates, 15 chairs, 1 looking glass, 5 guilt frames.* Evidently before "the British were coming," Cadwalader took away the five Peales on their stretchers! But Baron von Knyphausen was a small German gentleman of the old school. Next to *1 settee* missing from the back parlor his steward notes: *Major Knight aid de camp to Genl Howe has borrowed this and not returned. The people at his quarters probably know where it is.* Nobody got away with anything undetected in the stable, either, for at the bottom is a postscript: *Four waggon wheels & a single horse chair were in the stable, but the wheels have been claimed & taken away as their property by General Sir Wm Howe's servants, & the chair by Mr. Craigs of this city.*

Now going forward eight years to April 1, 1786, the collection holds another inventory (of main rooms and garret only)—this made for the late John Calwalader's estate by his sister and brother-in-law. In trunks in the attic they found ten blue damask chair covers and ten yellow damask chair bottoms, along with two blue and two yellow window curtains. We excerpt the chairs:

Back parlor	*10*	*mahogany*	*chairs*	
Front "	*10*	*"*	*"*	
Back chamber 2nd floor	*6*	*"*	*"*	*with chintz furniture*
Front " " "	*6*	*"*	*carpet bottom chairs*	
" room 3rd story	*2 old chairs 6 mahogany chairs*			
" garret	*10 old mahogany chairs many broke*			
	[50 total]			

This looks a bit simplistic and, sure enough, leaves us wondering what happened to Savery's nineteen walnut chairs. Here we're sorry to suspect that the signers, Rebecca Cadwalader and Samuel Meredith, didn't know walnut from mahogany. (Most people don't!) Trumble's twelve bowback Windsors are missing, too, but these at any rate wouldn't have stood in the formal rooms. Children's and kitchen chairs, as well as one with rockers added by Savery in 1772, are not mentioned. Probably some of these pieces were now lodged at Shrewsbury, the Kent County plantation house built by John Cadwalader in 1772.

That the twenty chairs in the townhouse parlors were the originals there is suggested by John Webster's bill of January 1772.* Webster was paid £2.16 *"To making 4 Silk Damask win Curtains lined &fringed"* and £2 for making twenty chair covers of *"Silk Damask."* These were the pieces found later in the attic. They must have been the cat's pajamas. The material came from the wholesale mercers Rushton & Beachcroft, 35 Grace Church Street, London, who on August 9, 1771, billed the General's agent there, Matthias Gale, a whopping £153.5.9 for a large order of damask plus trimmings. Presumably the twenty parlor chairs, which may or may not have been a single set, were among the thirty-two finished in canvas by Fleeson in 1770. At this time Fleeson was a principal upholsterer for Randolph.

But things have been going too smoothly here, for lately another student of this matter† has turned up Colonel Edward Lloyd's estate inventory at the HSP. It shows that ten mahogany side chairs, two matching armchairs, and six mahogany chairs from the *"Room over the Passage"* passed from Wye House to Betsy and John on the Colonel's death in January 1770.

*Webster supplied not only fine upholstery, but his own insecticide for delousing it:

JOHN WEBSTER, Upholsterer, From London, at the house occupied by Mr. William Rush, in Arch-street, near Second street, Begs leave to acquaint all ladies and gentlemen, and those who shall please to employ him in the Upholsterer's Business, that they may depend on having their work executed in the best and newest taste, such as sophas, couches, canopies, and canopy beds, French elbows, stools, chairs, rooms hung with paper, chintz, damask, or tapestry, &c. Also, the newest invented Venetian sun blinds for windows. . . . As said Webster had had the honour of working with applause, for several of the nobility and gentry in England and Scotland, hopes he will meet with a small degree of encouragement amongst the benevolent of Philadelphia, as they may depend on being punctually and reasonably served.

N.B. At said place may be had Webster's Liquor, for entirely destroying that offensive and destructive vermin called Buggs, which he has compleated with success.

—*Pennsylvania Journal,* August 20, 1767

† Beatrice B. Garvan, Philadelphia Museum of Art.

From all this documentation should emerge a large set of mahogany chairs identifiable as Randolph's or some other maker's, but instead each bit of new evidence expands the guessing game. No 18th-century bill or inventory even uses the word "set," and the truth of these details isn't apt to be symmetrical. General von Knyphausen left fifteen chairs *"In the large front parlour"* along with *4 tables—two mahagoni & two marble plates."* If these pieces formed all or part of the original suite, our ball game may be won. Knyphausen also records six chairs *"In the small front parlour,"* six *"In the back parlour,"* and sixty-five elsewhere (*"1 broke"*). Even agreeing, as we do, that the chairs from Wye made up some of the original furniture in Second Street, the situation's idiosyncrasies have simply escaped us. It looks reasonable, for example, to decide that Colonel Lloyd's ten side chairs were the ten standing in the back parlor in 1786, and perhaps they were—yet the fact is that this set with its two armchairs totaled twelve. We can just as well conclude that the Wye side chairs got pushed into the attic by then—*"10 old mahogany chairs many broke."* Chairs made for the Cadwaladers about 1770 weren't *"old"* by 1786.

Let's go back then to Fleeson's bill, dated at the beginning, October 18, 1770. Can we assume that fifteen or even twenty of these thirty-two chairs Fleeson covered *"over Rail"* may have been our hairy-paws? Yes, we can assume they may have been, but we don't *know*.

All in all, our attempts here to pin down the chairs in the parlors make us think of the scholar who spent his life trying to prove that Mozart was a Jew.

What could I take away from Philadelphia that I did know?

Well, then—

At least *one* chair of the Fanshawe series stood in that house.

4
Some Pieces That May Or May Not Fit

"They are the obvious suspects," said Miss Marple apologetically, "and the obvious, more often than not, is right."

—Agatha Christie,
The Mirror Crack'd from Side to Side

IN A DETECTIVE STORY the writer sets up events that at first can't be explained, and then in one way or another surprises the reader into seeing what he has seen from the start. If the mystery is a real-life one, so much the better.

Ours has been a real-life one, all right—only too real, for we haven't yet nailed down the solution to the case of the Fanshawe chairs and can now only suggest one that fits the incomplete evidence. Is this answer right? Our big surprise, then, is that we don't know. As the police like to put it, the investigation is continuing. Is this kind of climax fair to you? Do I presume too much? The truth is that I presume something more—the inadvertent photograph, letter, invoice, or other scrap of writing that will clear everything up is going to be produced finally by you. One of you, that is, out there. When and where will you find it? Again I can't say. God knows antiquarians and furniture historians move slowly. It took thirty years just to prove the sample chairs American! Lacking proof, my responsibility here is to give the negative as well as positive evidence. This puzzle, too, is going to yield not to logic but to more data.

For a moment this past winter, standing in the stacks at the Pennsylvania Historical Society, it seemed I'd stumbled on just this honor (and how deserved!). It was a brown envelope bearing English stamps and postmarked March 29, 1952. On it the sender wrote *From/ Mrs Charles Cadwalader/ 10. Richmond Mansions/ London* and to *Mrs John Cadwalader/ Broad Axe/ Ambler P.O./ Pennsylvania/ U.S.A.*

The envelope was tape-reinforced and stamped *Passed Free U.S. Customs at Philadelphia* and *Letter Package Collect Ten Cents*. The lettering had the labored clarity of an old person's; it didn't look like the handwriting on the chairs at all.

Inside was nothing.

But what the envelope had held lay in these stacks. Dr. Charles's commissions? Early letters, bits of his story or hers? I might find these bits at least, and match them, perhaps, with others. Also, London was too vast a city, but starting in the place of Mrs. Charles Calwalader's birth, did anyone remember?

Bridget Mary Ryan was born July 8, 1876. She came from Tipperary, a small market town east of Limerick. Travelers passing through see a line of shopfronts in stone houses along the main street, grubby but solid Victorian. This is about all they pause to see; the town is a highway junction branching northeast toward the Rock of Cashel and Dublin and south through the dairyland of County Tipperary. In town the highway and its shops run level along a slope—up on the side streets are St. Michael's Church, the Garda or police station, and lines of little row houses. The convent school the Ryan girls attended may be up there, too—I didn't see it. Downhill stands a no-nonsense hotel, the Royal, and across the valley lie an old parade ground and barracks that once billeted a unit of the British army; the parade ground is now a football field.

Tipperary lacks antiquities—its sole monument is of a bearded man sitting atop a plinth on the main street, *Charles J. Kickham—Poet, Novelist and above all Patriot*. Kickham belonged to the Young Ireland movement and in 1848 made pikes for the guerrilla fighters of Smith O'Brien. In prison he wrote a novel, *Sally Cavanagh, or the Untenanted Graves*. Through traffic has rumbled past his likeness for a long time.

The Hotel Royal was built long ago for commercial travelers in a place where there can be few commercial travelers. Such enticements as TV sets or waterbeds would look ridiculous there, but the common bathrooms on each floor, their white tiles spotless, are fitted with bathtubs of magnificent Sybaritic size, tubs that might receive the Cardiff Giant. In the Royal's entrance hang four early photographs maybe from Bridget Mary's time—Kickham sat there then, the street past him full of farm wagons and pedestrians in ankle-length dresses and black threadbare suits. Then, as now, the glory of this hard little town looked to be its children, pumped with life and spirit, bang-kneed and cheerful. Not here but in Cork, one of these small boys came along with a slotted tin can, collecting for God knows what. When I dropped in a coin, he cried, "Oh, isn't that *nice* of you!"

It's been written that Bridget Mary's people were "agriculturists" (Dr. Charles's word), which some of them may have been, but her father Michael Ryan and grandfather before him served as sergeants in the Royal Irish Constabulary, working in and out of the old stone Garda station up the hill. Her mother Mary came from Hospital, a village in County Limerick.

On July 15, 1897, the *Philadelphia Evening Bulletin* reported that the Ryans had four sons and four daughters, Bridget Mary being termed "a slight, tall, fair girl, with light brown hair and eyes, prettily chiselled features and a mobile countenance of singular refinement and beauty." Five years earlier, when there had been as yet no occasion for the *Bulletin*'s reporter to summon his descriptive powers, Bridget Mary had sailed at 16 for America with one of her older sisters. Probably they left from Queenstown, the seaport now called Cóbh. We know nothing of the details, though the dreadful grief of these family partings at the Cove of Cork is still planted in Irish memories. Thousands of those embarking here for Quebec, Montreal, Boston, New York, and Philadelphia must have been tired, poor, and yearning to breathe free—our guess is that Sergeant Ryan's girls were bright and strong and already breathing free!

Where Bridget Mary Ryan worked during her first three years in America we don't know. Her sister married, and at the end of 1895, looking to be a dressmaker, Bridget Mary went into an employment agency in Philadelphia. The lady who ran this "Intelligence Office" happened to be one of Dr. Charles Cadwalader's patients. She sent the applicant marching over to 240 South Fourth to replace a maid just fired for theft.

The house still stands, owned since 1912 by the Mutual Assurance Company, whose fire mark is *The Green Tree*. Here Dr. Charles, his brother John, and five sisters were raised. A few years after Dr. Charles inherited the place in 1889, the Sunday *Inquirer* ran a story on it:

> The present Cadwalader mansion in the old "Nobility Row" on Fourth Street was built about eighty years ago. To it the traditions, the relics and the remarkable series of portraits by Peale which adorned the old house were transferred, and it has more than kept up the reputation for hospitality and social supremacy which attached to the older one. Especially in the time of the late Judge John Cadwalader, the father of the

present representative of the family, and his beautiful wife, conceded to be "one of the most charming hostesses in Philadelphia," the splendor of the entertainments given there place it foremost in the list of noted mansions of Philadelphia.

The exterior of the house is plain, almost to Quaker severity, and hardly prepares the visitor for the extreme elegance and luxury within. It is an immense four-story double mansion of red brick, with the unusual architectural feature of two entrances, one at the extreme right and one at the extreme left of the building. Still another peculiarity which no other even of the old houses in the city exhibits, is apparent immediately the wide entrance doors are thrown open and the visitor enters the vestibule, as spacious as some drawing rooms are built in these days of tiny dwelling houses—a wide double stair-case, extending to the third story. The two stair-cases run parallel, the one behind the other, forming double landings all the way up, and were doubtless intended as a convenience in a house where so many entertainments were given, that the guests might enter by one set of stairs and depart by the other. . . .

Old-time relics of interest to the general public as well as to the historian and antiquarian, fill the house. Foremost among these is the noted collection of family portraits by Peale and Stuart, which are considered to be the finest works of the former in the portrait painting line. These portraits were brought to the Fourth Street house from the one on Second Street, where they occupied panels on the wall, and probably no family in Philadelphia has so complete a series of their ancestors' portraits. . . .

Facing the door is a large portrait of Dr. Thomas Cadwalader, son of the first Cadwalader, who came over to the new country with Penn. . . .

A portrait of his wife, a sweet faced dame in Quaker cap and kerchief, hangs beside that of their second son, Colonel Lambert Cadwalader, who took up his residence in West Jersey and whose Revolutionary services as a Trenton citizen were gracefully acknowledged by the recent act of City Council's in naming "Cadwalader Park", in Trenton, after him.

Another portrait presents a pretty family group, General John Cadwalader, of the Continental Army, his wife and child. General Cadwalader was a close personal friend of Washington, who spoke of him as "a military genius" and named him as a suitable successor in the chief command in the event of his own disablement. His "Greens", or "Silk Stocking Company", a battalion not unlike our present City Troop in its personnel, was the first company organized for defense in the Revolution. The women of the Cadwalader family are represented by portraits of Mrs. Dagworthy (Martha Cadwalader) and Lady Erskine (Frances Cadwalader), whose husband, the son of Lord Chancellor Erskine, was English Minister to the United States. Both women were beautiful, Lady Erskine in especial. . . .

With this the *Inquirer* ran drawings from photographs of the house-front, as well as of one front hall and the dining room. The dining room chairs, alas, are framed ones with slip seats, actually American Empire and of no distinction. Presumably this is the set catalogued later as "*Ten Handsome Antique Mahogany Chairs*." If so, they did well to make $180! Wainwright has published an 1889 photo of the parlor—the sole visible heirloom is the Met's marble-top pier table. Of the other formal rooms and four main bedrooms, the latter reported to be furnished in old mahogany,* we've found no photographs. That earlier the back bed-chamber held at least one Chippendale heirloom we know also from Mrs. Rowland's leaving her pier glass there.

But we've left Bridget Mary standing at the door. Events are now unfolded by Hartley Davis, a feature writer for the Philadelphia *World*, who came around to interview the bridegroom on July 23, 1897. His account, with drawings of the happy couple and the dining room, ran two days later, headlined THE HEAD OF THE FOREMOST FAMILY IN AMERICA WEDS HIS SERVING MAID. After warming up with Dr. Charles's pedigree and accomplishments, Davis reports:

> Dr. Cadwalader was conscious of the fact that in Bridget Ryan he had secured an admirable servant. During the first year that she was in his employ Dr. Cadwalader thinks that he did not address one hundred words to her, all told.
>
> Each year Dr. Cadwalader has been in the habit of giving three or four set entertainments. By far the most important is his New Year's reception, when all the members of the family and about a dozen intimate friends who are closely connected with it are bidden to his house. Just prior to this he places the great establishment in order. It has been his custom to add new decorations; he has carried out his ideas himself. Now, it happened that while this housecleaning was going on Dr. Cadwalader needed the services of one of his servants. Bridget Ryan came to his aid. There was a difference of opinion upon a certain matter, of itself unimportant.
>
> Then it was that Dr. Cadwalader first noticed Bridget Ryan. He saw before him a young woman tall and slender. She wore the plainest of gowns and her figure was remarkably graceful. He saw that her hands were admirably shaped. He looked at her head with the scrutiny of a scientific man. He saw a broad, almost square forehead surmounted by a great mass of reddish brown hair, beautiful rebellious hair. He noticed

**The Evening Bulletin*, July 16, 1897.

particularly that her head was well shaped. He came to the conclusion then that it was the best shaped head that he had ever seen, and was amazed to perceive also that the features of his serving maid were almost classic.

She had been his waiting maid for a year, but he had never before looked at her.

He entered into conversation with her, she working the while. He noticed that her hands and her mind were in perfect accord. He was impressed by the fact that she had an innate refinement and a simple, natural dignity. She appeared to be wholesome and good. She spoke a delicious brogue that sounded more Scotch than Irish.

As a matter of fact the old bachelor fell in love with this girl on the spot, but he did not realize it until long after. But he was sensible of her charm and fascination. The more he talked with her the more he was impressed with her excellent qualities. And above all she seemed to fit so perfectly into the household. In this connection came the thought that he might lose her, and this filled the doctor with alarm. It seemed to him another instance of that special Providence which had guarded his life that Bridget Ryan should have been brought into his home.

. . . Inside of a month after Dr. Cadwalader had his first conversation with his serving maid he knew that he was head over heels in love with her. But his infatuation did not blind his judgement or reason. Above all things Dr. Cadwalader is a reasoning man. . . . He knew that his relatives and Philadelphia society would be aghast at the thought of his marrying a housemaid in his own service. . . .

As a matter of fact this question, important as it was, did not trouble Dr. Cadwalader half so much as the fear that Bridget Ryan could not love him. She was not yet twenty-one and he was fifty-seven.

All women who have met Dr. Cadwalader like him. And it is easy to understand how Bridget Ryan could love him. He has an air of distinction. He has the fine, strong nose which is the mark of the Cadwaladers. He has the face of an aristocrat.

He has the most beautiful manners, that "pineapple perfume of politeness", the courtliness, the gallantry that seems to be met with nowadays only among men whose hair is white. And Dr. Cadwalader never impresses those who know him with the fact that he is fifty-seven years old. His movements have the elasticity, the quickness and he has the alert air of a man of thirty. To-day there is nothing he enjoys more than a hard game of cricket. He was the founder of the Germantown Cricket Club. . . .

It was natural enough that Bridget Ryan should look upon her employer with a feeling that was akin to love, but she was a very much startled young woman when he asked her to marry him. He proposed to

—Philadelphia *World,* July 25, 1897

MISS BRIDGET RYAN,
The serving maid from Tipperary, whom Dr. Cadwalader has just married (from a photograph).

—Philadelphia *World*, July 25, 1897

his serving maid as he would to a grande dame. And this serving maid accepted him with a native dignity and a fluttering happiness that filled him with joy.

The doctor went forth and told the members of his family about it. His relatives showed signs of going stark, staring mad on the spot; but after he talked with them a while they behaved very well indeed.

The doctor is the head of the family, you know, not only in name, but in fact. He told them that he was marrying a good, wholesome, honest girl, upon whose name there was no shadow and who would make a much better wife than many society women he knew. With a scientific man's bluntness, he said that it was wise to have new and vigorous blood infused into the family.

Other people in the social swim, when they heard about the engagement, did not believe a word of it. It was really impossible to conceive of a Cadwalader marrying a servant girl. The doctor pursued his way evenly. There was little change in the household except where he formerly addressed his maid as "Bridget" he now called her Miss Ryan.

They were engaged five months. During this time Bridget Ryan continued to perform her household duties as she did before. The only difference was that in the evenings she chatted with the doctor in the library. She was formally introduced to his friends who called.

These would have been happy months had not the religious question intervened. Dr. Cadwalader had written to Bridget's father a very courteous, formal and respectful request for the daughter's hand in marriage. There came in return a reply written in such admirable taste that the doctor was surprised and delighted.

The doctor and Bridget Ryan had talked over the religious question and it was understood between them that when she was his wife she should attend St. Paul's Episcopal Church, of which Dr. Cadwalader is an officer, in the morning, and go to her own church, Roman Catholic, in the afternoon.

St. Mary's Catholic Church is next door to the doctor's residence. He and Rev. Father McDermott have always been warm friends, each respecting the other's honesty, sincerity and earnestness in their opposing religious beliefs.

The order came from the parish priest in Tipperary that Dr. Cadwalader must agree that the children should be raised in the Catholic faith. He was up in arms at once. He looked upon this as an infraction upon his personal liberty. It looked very much as if there would be no wedding. Bridget Ryan saw the difficulty. She determined in her own mind to leave her own church for that of her prospective husband.

Dr. Cadwalader made very sure that the young woman was ready to make the sacrifice without reservation and without violation of her conscience. This was the only real obstacle to the marriage.*

The preparations for the wedding were few. Dr. Cadwalader insisted that his bride should have new gowns. Her wedding dress was a simple travelling one. In the morning the doctor attended a meeting of a charitable organization. After luncheon he went to the County Clerk's office and took out his license.

Then he walked home, tucked Bridget Ryan under his arm, and they walked a couple of blocks to St. Paul's Church, where they were married about 3 P.M. on July 15. After the wedding they walked out of the church, took the trolley car and rode to the Pennsylvania station. They boarded a train for New York and went to the Fifth Avenue Hotel.

They were away from Philadelphia about a week. When he returned home Dr. Cadwalader found hundreds of letters from his friends congratulating him upon his courage in marrying in defiance of social convention.

Bridget Ryan, the Irish immigrant girl, left the house a servant and returned to it its mistress. She was no longer Bridget Ryan, but Mrs. Charles Ebert Cadwalader, whose husband is the head of the foremost family in America, and who would be the social leader if he chose to exercise his prerogative.

The girl who came to America in the steerage was the mistress of the finest old Colonial mansion in Philadelphia. It has stood in Fourth Street, between Locust and Spruce, for nearly a hundred years. In it is all the furniture, pictures, silver and china that was brought from the older mansion, which was on Second street, where it occupied a whole block.†

She can sit on chairs that Washington, Adams, Jefferson and all the great men of the Revolution occupied, for there was not one who was not entertained in the old Cadwalader mansion. She can live in the rooms occupied by proud and aristocratic women of the Cadwalader race,

*On the sore point of religious jurisdiction the *Philadelphia Evening Bulletin* for July 15, 1897 says that Bridget Mary's father "sought the advice of Father Keeley, the village priest at Tipperary. Affidavits of consent were drawn up by a Limerick notary and were sent to the doctor by Mr. and Mrs. Ryan. Interesting letters accompanied them, giving family blessing, etc." However, when the affianced couple would not bind their children to Catholicism "the Tipperary priest was far from pleased. He wrote to the church authorities in America, protesting and appealing to Father McDermott to forbid the banns." The question was then put to the Philadelphia archbishop.

I lately called on the rector of St. Michael's in Tipperary, Archdeacon Ryan, but he could find no record of *our* Ryan. Ryans were everywhere, and Americans who wrote him were forever confusing County Tipperary with Tipperary town. But this error I managed to escape, for when I asked the archdeacon who was rector there in 1897, he spelled, "*Kieley*."

†Actually the house measured 41 by 38 feet, without its kitchen wing.

women who had lived in the fashionable world for generations. Bridget Ryan is their successor.

She neither asked nor interested herself about the greeting she would receive from the people of Philadelphia, who are so bound by caste. She seems to have no social ambitions.

Dr. Cadwalader knows what the result will be. Society will receive Mrs. Charles Ebert Cadwalader, who was Bridget Ryan, housemaid. Society will receive Mrs. Cadwalader because her husband says it shall be so. The members of his family will take the initiative. If the Cadwaladers set the seal on a prizefighter he would be admitted to the best society in Philadelphia.

They will attend and give a few receptions in order that Mrs. Cadwalader's place may be permanently fixed, and then will no doubt retire into their own quiet and happy existence.

The strangest thing of all in this remarkable romance is the place that Mrs. Cadwalader now occupies in the household. She is still the maid, so far as the domestic duties are concerned. She has not changed her life in the slightest degree. She still wears simple gowns. She still dusts the fine pieces of mahogany. She still waits on the doctor at breakfast, luncheon and dinner as she did when she was plain Bridget Ryan. This is her wish, and Dr. Cadwalader permits her to have her way, saying that if she wishes to follow a German custom she may do so.

A few nights ago Miss Sarah Cadwalader, his eldest sister, dined with him, and Mrs. Cadwalader waited upon them, as she had many times before. . . .

As she serves her husband seated at the table, portraits of his ancestors look down upon her. . . . There is a picture there, too, of a daughter of the house, a picture painted by Gilbert Stuart, of her who became Lady Erskine, and whose descendants are peers in England to-day.

The serving-maid, the daughter of an Irish constable, who has become the wife of Dr. Cadwalader, may look upon this portrait of Lady Erskine and know that her children will not only have the heritage of a great name, but that they will be blood kin to Sir William Erskine, the Duke of Portland and to the Duke of Argyle.

Yes, well, shades of the penny thrillers—and, even nicer, of *Jane Eyre* and *Mansfield Park*!

Dr. Charles left quite a bit of material about himself, yet it's not so easy to make him out. Reversing the usual pattern, he seems to have started out conforming and later gone his own way. Graduating from the College of Physicians at the University of Pennsylvania in 1861, he delayed practicing medicine, choosing to go off to war instead with the Philadelphia City Troop.*

He took with him into the Army his great grandfather's instinct for the levers of command. On an old order detailing him to headquarters staff of the Army of the Potomac, Dr. Charles has noted: "I was transferred to General Meade's staff by his request on the 28th June 1863 at the time of Genl Hooker's being relieved from Command of the Army—I had previously served on Genl Hookers staff from March 17th 1863." The next year he was back in the line as Captain, Company D, 6th Pennsylvania Cavalry, and in 1865 on Hooker's recommendation was promoted to Brevet Major "for distinguished gallantry and meritorious services at the Battle of Chancellorsville." As the Confederacy at last neared collapse, Stanton, the Secretary of War, commissioned him a Brevet Lieutenant Colonel for gallantry at the Battle of Gettysburg and in the "campaign from the Rapidan to the James in 1864." These actions far exceeded the 1777 morning at Princeton in their horror and carnage. As it all ended, Dr. Charles was 26.

He accepted a political sinecure as Clerk of the Bankruptcy Court in Philadelphia, his father John Cadwalader (1805–79) then sitting as a Federal judge appointed by President Buchanan. Apparently he was now pressed into service by many a hostess, though declining always to offer the supreme sacrifice. In 1871, his sister Fannie suffered a nervous breakdown and Dr. Charles took her to Europe. When Fannie died—and after eight years or so of personal drift—he joined the staff of the Episcopal Hospital and finally took up practicing medicine. Judging from the press accounts, Dr. Charles proved an able and compassionate physician who didn't care whether his patients paid him or not. After his father died, he went on living at South Fourth Street with his mother, until in 1889 she was gone too. He wasn't so young any more, and the great house with its contents was now his.

He declined two legacies from his uncle, which, he told his alarmed kin, would be sown broadcast in favor of the poor. The Cadwaladers knew what it was to be poor—that had happened to one or two of them before and wasn't really a laughing matter. Besides calling on the sick and dispossessed Dr. Charles evidently passed quite a bit of time at

*The elite First City Troop was put into armored vehicles in World War II, and is now a unit of the 28th Infantry Division, Pennsylvania National Guard.

home with his stuffed peacock and other oddments, brooding and fiddling. But he greeted each day with pep and exercise. He kept in the pink of health. Even at 57 (actually 58), Hartley Davis noted, Dr. Charles was "no dotard whose trembling mind is swayed by a young and pretty face. He is the youngest man of his years in Philadelphia. Every muscle in his body is developed like that of a professional athlete. He possesses prodigious strength and activity. Probably not one man in a thousand could hold his own against Dr. Cadwalader in a hand-to-hand fight."

Exactly what was his problem? Jane Austen would have admired Dr. Charles, too, and she seems to have had someone like him in mind in 1813 when she wrote, "It is a truth universally acknowledged, that a single man in possession of a good fortune must be in want of a wife."

For many years Dr. Charles didn't want one at all, and now it was nearly too late. On her side, Bridget Mary came to him dowered with a serene spirit and even a turn for happiness. The cook called her "Brightie, a nickname appropriate to her sunny, cheerful disposition."

But they miscalculated. They misjudged the nature of Philadelphia society, that brave old turkey buzzard just now at this writing being driven from its roost in the Bellevue Stratford Hotel. Their union wounded those about them in a way they didn't at first understand. Family and property, property and family—had he really meant to dump them by the road? To commit, after all, this grotesquerie? While the General misbehaved back in 1778, he kept Anne Dingwell in a different house, at last leaving her and their daughter Sarah a small income. Now instead Dr. Charles turned into the wind.

The rock they struck seems to have been his younger brother, John Cadwalader (1843–1925). Banker John followed his father in reading law at the University of Pennsylvania. Now he was president of two shipping lines, the Trust Company of North America, and the city's University Club. After Dr. Charles's rather cavalier rejection of his uncle's fortune, Banker John accepted it with good grace. His widowed aunt in turn left him the house at 1519 Locust Street, which held among other things the hairy-paw card table. To Banker John the table must have been the least of it. With Bridget Mary's coup the patrimony of the senior line was carved away from his son, a young man also named John Cadwalader (1874–1934). What Banker John could do, about this and all the gossip, was nothing. Apparently that's what he did. He didn't call again at the house where he was born.

Charles E. Cadwalader, Pennsylvania Cavalry, 1861
—Historical Society of Pennsylvania

As the years passed, things might have mended. The brothers, who lived just a few blocks apart, took to sending each other letters, but only their correspondence prospered. On July 2, 1903, Dr. Charles sent over a long, long one. It disputed who gave the family portraits to whom—while the writer had always borne the interests of John's children in mind, the tenor of his twenty or more closely reasoned pages was that the Charles E. Cadwaladers didn't plan to be ducked in the bath, either.

That winter Bridget Mary had a quiet announcement to make; she was expecting. Their baby was born the following July, 1904. His parents chose to name him John Biddle Cadwalader.

Hartley Davis's forecast of smooth sailing for the newlyweds proved sanguine. For thirty years Dr. Charles had found the Old Guard's assemblies and pretensions a bore and in 1897, it seemed, had contrived to publicly declare their daughters the same. They could repay him only with silence. Having borne it with patience and fortitude for seven years, the Charles Cadwaladers now gave up.

That summer they prepared their surprise.

Bridget Mary had never seen London, but Dr. Charles may have stopped there when he took his sister Fannie abroad in 1871. Why London? We don't know. Because they might float on that wide sea of civility far away, because one of the Ryans was established there? That they planned more than a tour is clear from the legend on the Davis & Harvey catalogue, which states that their goods are "*To be sold by order of Dr. Chas. E. Cadwalader, prior to his residence in Europe*." And that this curious little émigré family headed by a 65-year-old physician would need to set up housekeeping in London is evident, even had they not taken along the family silver. Between all this and the baby's arrival they must have had a time of it that summer. Among the countless things to be done it looks reasonable, though far from certain, that having chosen five prize chairs from the bedrooms for their London household, they now had them reupholstered by John Wanamaker's.

(If they didn't, who did?)

Did Charles Hanlon come to South Fourth Street? Or were the chairs taken to him? We have no clue. Apparently after recovering them and "signing" his work, at any rate, he fitted the splat shoes again over the new fabric.

The portraits posed a sticky problem. Dr. Charles's ambivalent attitude toward the family heritage didn't quite extend to forever denying his brother's and sisters' children the sight of their ancestors' likenesses, yet there was now John Biddle to consider. Nobody was such an oaf any longer to appraise one of these five triumphant Peales at $2. There were also the Thomas Sully of the General's only son Thomas, two Erskine portraits by Gilbert Stuart, a doubtful Stuart of Williamina Bond's brother, and a portrait of Major General George Cadwalader (1806–79), the Judge's brother, by a local artist whose name was now being heard, Thomas Eakins. Dr. Charles decided to lend the whole lot to the Pennsylvania Historical Society, along with the Washington letters he still had. He'd earlier given some of the letters to the city of Philadelphia to be kept in Independence Hall Museum.

The sale was well advertised, although it looks as if on opening day, November 3, only Mrs. Henry J. Rowland (the Doctor's sister) appeared from the family. Neither the owner nor his brother showed up. Dr. Charles explained, "I have no time to give to the sale, and I don't know what sort of prices the things are bringing. My wife and I will be out of town until election day, and as soon as I have voted we will start for Italy." He added gratuitously, "I don't believe in surrendering my franchise rights for the sake of getting to Italy a week or two earlier."

Also he wanted his proceeds from Davis & Harvey's, which the next week came to about $14,000.

After the Chinese export porcelain and cut glass were sold, the mahogany began to come up, and James Curran successfully bid $450 for Lot 168, "*Handsome Antique Console Table, profusely carved, scroll legs, Egyptian marble top.*" On November 8, *The North American* published a drawing of the table together with a lamp, firescreen, the Cadwalader cradle, and a tin foot tub.

A detailed story on the second day's action ran in *The Evening Bulletin* that same date, November 4:

CADWALADER RELICS BRING HIGH PRICES

"H", a Mysterious Bidder, Buys in a
Carved Colonial Chair for $160
After Sharp Bargaining

IS THE FAMILY BIDDING?

> Prices fluctuated strangely at the second day's sale of the furniture and collection of antiques from the home of Dr. Charles E. Cadwalader, at Davis & Harvey's auction rooms today. The gallery was crowded with purchasers and the merely curious, but there was not the representation of Philadelphia fashionables so noticeable when the sale began yesterday.
>
> Many of the dealers present bought heavily, and at prices which preclude the possibility of their disposing of the antiques again at a profit. From this it was judged that they were buying for members of the family who were desirous of retaining some of the historic heirlooms. One dealer concealed his identity with the initial "H" and made several purchases after spirited bargaining. He was unknown to the local dealers and refused to say where he was from.
>
> The highest price obtained for any of the pieces was $160. This was paid by the mysterious "H" for a handsomely carved chair, said to have been made for John Cadwalader in colonial times. Another chair of the same sort, but with plain legs and sadly in need of upholstering, was bought by the same dealer for $85. An odd boot and shoe rack also went to "H" for $34, but he was outbid by Mrs. Silas W. Pettit when two side-arm chairs with torn yellow satin covering were put up.
>
> The bidding started at $25 and climbed in $5 jumps to $90 each. Three interested purchasers stopped nodding their heads after the half century mark was reached, and the bidding was confined to Mrs. Pettit and a local dealer. He studied his catalogue too long when he had nodded to the auctioneer's "$85 I am bid", and Mrs. Pettit advanced the price another five dollars. When the chairs were knocked down to her she exclaimed gleefully to a companion: "We've saved our chairs, anyhow." Mrs. Pettit also purchased lacquered glass lamp shades and a pair of beautifully decorated Chinese porcelain garden stools. She paid $11 for the stools.

Those on the floor were then surprised that the ancestral cradle brought only $8. A period tip-top table (Lot 235. "*Large antique mahogany turnover centre table, finely carved column and claw feet, beautiful stave top of San Domingo mahogany.*") made $150. Then:

> More interest was manifested when the ten mahogany framed chairs* that accompanied the table were put up. They were started at $5 each, and climbed rapidly until $19 was reached. The dealer who got the table said $18 was his limit, and the chairs, with their horsehair upholstery, were sold to a stylishly dressed woman who refused to give her name.

The peacock that had stood at the head of the stairs made $12 and

*Catalogued as "*Ten Handsome Antique Mahogany Chairs; scroll legs, upholstered in Canary satin damask.*"

somebody paid $3.50 for a musical bird in a cage. At last the stereopticon with a missing lens found a new owner, and it was over. Dr. Charles had worked his will. Probably the finest collection of American Chippendale furniture ever made for one house and family had been scattered to the winds.

Davis & Harvey's didn't spend any superlatives on the "ten mahogany framed chairs," and at $18 apiece they could not have been comparable to the one that made $160. What of this carved chair that "H" carried away? Might it be the very one in Lambert's portrait and the only chair of this design ever owned by the Cadwaladers? It's possible. Yet it's a little hard to imagine that a person unknown had the Fanshawes made, while John Cadwalader commissioned the making of his card table to match a single chair. The card game would need to have been solitaire.

The only two pieces we can identify as single mahogany side chairs are given in the catalogue as:

> *Lot 280. "Elegant antique mahogany chair, carved back, scroll legs and ball and claw feet."*
> *Lot 284. "Handsome antique mahogany chair, carved back, tapestry seat."*

We believe this last chair the one for which "H" paid $85, since the "plain legs" mentioned in the *Bulletin* are indicated in the catalogue by omission of "*scroll*," or cabriole, legs. All the hairy-paws are on "scroll" legs.

On its face, the description of Lot 280 eliminates the hairy-paw chairs, because the feet are given as *"ball and claw."* But we'd better reflect that in 1904 the term "hairy-paw" was heard mostly around a zoo. The cataloguer seems to describe the hairy-paw furniture in this consignment simply as having "*claw feet.*" We can accept Lot 280 as a hairy-paw chair, then, only if the catalogue is flatly in error. Possibly it is.

We are looking at rather misty signals here, but then if this was a suspense novel, everybody wouldn't be named John Cadwalader.

John Biddle Cadwalader, only a few months old, accompanied his parents to London via Italy. It seems most unlikely that they moved right into 10 Richmond Mansions, but we have no clue to where they did settle. Their heavy belongings, including the silver and any furniture Dr. Charles saved, may have been shipped directly to England.

The little family lived together over there for two and a half years, then it was suddenly and totally destroyed. On March 9, 1907, John

Biddle died, not quite three. His father insisted on sending the baby's body back to Philadelphia, though he found himself unable to go with it. Somebody (perhaps her sister) wrote Bridget Mary that to the small funeral at Christ Church on Second Street her brother-in-law's son, John Cadwalader, Jr., came with flowers. This gesture Bridget Mary didn't forget. Less than two months later, on June 12, Dr. Charles died, too.*

He willed his entire estate to his wife.

At 31, Bridget Mary found herself a widow alone in London, but by no means penniless. Apparently in that city she remained for half a century.

Had she gone home to live in Tipperary, probably we'd have been able to pick up her trail, but neither the Garda Siochana nor Archdeacon Ryan there knew her name. One of the Garda at the station was good enough to telephone around town for us, but touched only one faint spark—an old man of 90 living on St. Michael's Street remembered that Sergeant Ryan's wife came from Hospital. The old man couldn't come to the phone, or see us.

In 1908, Bridget Mary gave all eighteen family portraits to her husband's nephew John Cadwalader, Jr. He hung some, including the Peale of the General's family, in his father's house on Locust Street. The Washington letters, whose manuscript value is now hard to estimate, she gave to the Historical Society of Pennsylvania. For a quarter century we hear nothing more of Dr. Charles's widow; then, in the 1930s, a case of silver arrived from London. Among the plate was a great half-gallon tankard bearing the maker's marks of William Penstone, London, 1712. This tankard weighed in at 42 ounces when the General died in 1786. It now passed by lot to its present owner, Captain John's brother Henry (the boy who recognized the card table in the painting). The rest of the plate was shared by Dr. Charles's other half dozen great nephews and nieces. The empty envelope from 10 Richmond Mansions shows that Bridget Mary was mailing memorabilia back to Captain John's mother in Ambler as late as 1952. The envelope is our last trace of her.

If Bridget Mary owned the Fanshawe chairs, she sold them before 1933, when Westmeath died.

We haven't a scrap of evidence suggesting they ever met, but the

*Dr. Charles and his son are buried in the Cadwalader vault at Christ Church Cemetery, Fifth and Arch Streets, Philadelphia. The church record gives John Biddle's age as "2½ yrs. & 2 mo."

similarities in the situations of these two seem interesting. Anthony Nugent was six years older. Although they were raised in very different homes 50 miles apart, from 1907 both frequented London as well-to-do absentee Irish, both single and both socially mobile. Both owned or had owned a good deal of Chippendale furniture, but Mrs. Charles Cadwalader's need for it diminished while Nugent found himself still improving his country seat into the 1920s.

Whatever her husband left her, the fact is that Bridget Mary was a long way from being the richest Cadwalader. By the time World War I ended, that distinction was gained by another family widow, Emily Roebling Cadwalader,* whose husband Richard had been one of Lambert's grandsons. He was a lawyer and president of the Philadelphia Club. After he died in 1918, Mrs. Richard owned a yacht named the *Alder* which was 294 feet long and cost about $175,000 a year to run. Her boat had antique tapestries on the saloon bulkheads, a large pipe organ, and gold-plated toilet fixtures. When Mrs. Richard sold the *Alder* to Mrs. William Boyce Thompson for $1,800,000, she decided to buy something a little more commodious for $2,500,000—the *Savarona*, at 408 feet the largest yacht in America.† *Savarona's* appointments, too, must have differed a bit from the berth assigned Bridget Mary back in 1892 at the Cove of Cork!

Bridget Mary and Westmeath may have known each other, but the arithmetic doesn't encourage us. You don't walk down Oxford Street in London without marveling at the vast human circuitry of this city. New Bond Street, a narrow one, runs into Oxford. Sotheby's here has very little street frontage—its old "rooms" look quite different from the modern plate glass of its Madison Avenue annex. Inside it's a warren and rabbit run of a place, with *cul de sacs*, narrow backstairs, and side rooms wonderful for exchanging confidences, if any. The salesrooms, too, are understated.

Did the chairs pass through here not once but twice?

Does this auction house or Christie's, or possibly the Victoria and Albert Museum, hold an old marked-up catalogue showing that a set of mahogany chairs (described erroneously as Georgian) were consigned for sale between 1907 and 1933 by Mrs. Charles Cadwalader? If so, we can be pretty sure the purchaser was Anthony Francis Nugent.

*The Roeblings of Trenton pioneered the modern suspension bridge, using cable of their own manufacture to hang the Brooklyn Bridge.

†Ferdinand Lundberg, *America's 60 Families* (New York: Vanguard, 1937).

Again the arithmetic looks difficult. Auctioneers, as we've learned, don't regard themselves as archivists, keepers of paper memorabilia. My guess was that the next break might come instead from somebody in County Kildare, Berks (England), Pennsylvania, or even a nursing home in Ocala, Florida—from somebody who doesn't throw old letters or photos away! It might, as George Stapleton suggested, start us in a whole new direction. Meanwhile, it was pleasant to imagine that the hairy-paw chairs no longer stood quite as bare as the shafts of the stone circle at Tynagh.

5
Some Pieces That Fit Perfectly, But

An answer is always a form of death.
—John Fowles, *The Magus*

THE TRIAL BY FIRE of the Bridget Mary Ryan story opened sooner than I'd expected.

When Queen Elizabeth II visited the Philadelphia Museum of Art on July 6, 1976, I was foolish enough to follow her down there next day, not so much out of an infatuation with royalty (but aren't they great?) but because one of the pieces loaned to the show was Fanshawe chair VIII. Beatrice Garvan, the museum's associate curator who chose and catalogued most of the 18th-century furniture, had agreed to see me at eleven, and I offered to trade her the gist of my Irish travels. But at that hour the meeting she was in did what meetings do, dragged on. The delay gave me a chance to look around and to read Garvan's observations in the catalogue.*

Chair VIII stood on a low platform, freshly covered with silk and refinished, barbered to the nines. (At the Met's show in New York, chair VII was turned out the same way—they just can't leave them alone!) Also up there stood the General's serpentine table, the family portrait you know about hanging above it, a crowd stopper. Out of the blue and added to our little shrine was a second card table—apparently an identical twin to the General's, except that the cabochon and leaf centered in its skirt curved in opposite directions.

Where did this come from? I'd never seen it before and found only the day before that it existed. It was loaned by the Dietrich Corporation of Reading, Pennsylvania, a company that is connected in a way I didn't

**Philadelphia: Three Centuries of American Art*, Bicentennial Exhibition, April 11 to October 10, 1976 (Philadelphia Museum of Art, 1976).

ask about with Mr. and Mrs. H. Richard Dietrich, Jr., of Chester Springs, Pennsylvania. The late dealer and antiquarian Charles Woolsey Lyon of Millbrook, New York, was the table's former owner. Lyon evidently didn't know where it came from, either, because he advertised it for sale in *Antiques* some years ago as a mate to the Cadwalader card table but without any family provenance. The Dietrich Company's curator Alexandra Garfield has since advised: "The table was bought from Charles Lyon but at that time he offered no details on provenance other than a vague reference to Nova Scotia."

The Queen, we were told, hadn't paid much attention to any of these high-style pieces—they had them back at the palace. What she liked most were her namesakes, the American Windsor chairs!

At any rate the Bicentennial celebration had finally detonated and now the city of Philadelphia lay strewn with wadding, as if an artillery barrage had been fired. President Ford and Her Majesty thanked Mayor Rizzo and left. Up on the Tappan Zee Bridge over the Hudson a long line of horse-drawn vehicles, the Bicentennial Wagon Train, crossed slowly, delaying traffic. When a TV cameraman stuck his lens in the face of a fat motorist stalled in the tie-up, the driver said, "What happened in 1776 I don't care."

At last Beatrice Garvan came out apologizing, and I followed her down to her office, really a collection of cubicles housing the staff of the American Arts department, awash like a publisher's office with overloaded desks, tables, filing cases, and people who'd missed their lunch. Even so, both here and upstairs they seemed such a happy crew—maybe because they'd just weathered the Bicentennial—that I felt a little mean about some of the things I've said about their fair city. I asked Garvan if she was connected to the Francis P. Garvans and she said she was their daughter-in-law. She was quite young and rangey looking in the way some tennis players are. When she began to talk, it was clear she was not only nice but as smart as a whip. So far as I know, she's the first furniture critic to discover (*Antiques*, July 1976) that the famed Randolph wing chair at that moment on the platform upstairs not only suffers from crude joinery but is "atypical of the Philadelphia style."

I had never liked the damned chair but was afraid to say so.

The museum had just been shut down—closed to the public—for about a year, getting itself overhauled and this show mounted. Its catalogue looked like the Manhattan phone book. The main thrust of

Garvan's research hadn't been the Fanshawes *per se*—in fact, she misspells the Major's name—but Benjamin Randolph and his carvers. I didn't have to read many lines to see she had scored a breakthrough on Randolph. Among other things, and I'd like to know how, she'd found a Randolph account book for 1768-87, stacked until lately unidentified in the manuscript room of the New York Public Library (NYPL card file *Philadelphia Merchant's Account Book, 1768-87*). Nowhere in the ledger's hundred-odd pages does Benjamin Randolph's name appear, though it's his, verified by Garvan's cross-checking entries with his receipt book at Winterthur and Captain John Macpherson's in the Philadelphia Museum. The recently discovered ledger doesn't list specific pieces of furniture, but it changes our idea of Randolph—he was not only in cabinetmaking and real estate, but lumbering and sawmill operations, shipping, and by 1779 even privateering.

As Woodhouse long ago suspected, Randolph hired Hercules Courtenay as a journeyman carver soon after he arrived (or returned) from London before 1765. He shortly took on another one, John Pollard, also sophisticated in his trade. The Winterthur receipt book shows that Randolph paid Pollard's house rent in December 1765 and again the next July. Garvan gives the carving in the Met's marble-top pier table to John Pollard. Her attribution is based largely on the chinoiserie, or imitation Chinese, flavor of this table's central figure—a Buddhalike creature holding a bird—which was probably Pollard's kind of thing, since he soon set up his own shop under the "Sign of the Chinese Shield." Linking Pollard to the pier table in this way seemed to me a bit thin (the pot calling the kettle black!), but Garvan goes on to find the executed style of Fanshawe chair VIII's rococo forms, really its carver's technique, more like this marble-top table's than that of the two serpentine card tables. She then gives the carving in chair VIII to Pollard, and that in the Cadwalader and Dietrich card tables to Courtenay. In the case of Courtenay, at least, architectural carving believed to be his has survived from the Powel house interior.

Then comes her blockbuster. In London during 1758-59 Chippendale & Rannie turned out a matched set of two serpentine card tables, two settees, and fourteen armchairs for Dumfries House, Ayrshire, Scotland. The tables resembled the pair here, although these looked to Garvan to follow even more closely the pinched knees and sweeping curves shown in Thomas Johnson's *One Hundred & Fifty New Designs*

(London, 1761). This grand idea of furnishing a room *en suite* with matching card tables and chairs was just the ticket for John Cadwalader.*

Another such suite we've since found painted by William Hogarth into his hilarious *Shortly After Marriage*, one of the *Marriage a la Mode* series. Here the master and mistress recover from their revels amid a set of at least eight upholstered Queen Anne side chairs and two matching card tables bearing the stubs, presumably stinking, of candle ends. Ensembles like this made in London were not by the late 1760s welcome in Philadelphia because of the Non-Importation Agreement signed by many resisters to the Crown. The signers of the 1765 embargo included both Cadwalader brothers and their father. And now—maybe—Benjamin Randolph turned out the samples to fill just this lack.

Beatrice Garvan talked with an offhand air, though obviously retracing a thread that had led her through many a thicket. As she went she dipped into her large and rather disorderly collection of index cards, letters, photos, and Xerox copies—shopping lists on which this precarious structure had been erected and now swayed just perceptibly. She had some new stuff.

They'd had quite a time of it this past year. Apparently getting it up for this big show had been something of a Chinese fire drill. The catalogue research alone looked exhaustive. In the past few weeks hardly anybody had any time with their families. This I believed. How did she get out for even a box of milk? Presently the phone rang, one of her daughters on the line.

"You're broke?" Garvan said. "You're bored? Oh, you're *bored*!"

Her catalogue material mentioned a seventh "sample" chair now in the Princeton University Art Museum, and I asked about it. Where did they come off calling that one a sample? She brought out a photo of it.

"This isn't one of the sample chairs," I said.

"Well, it's Randolph's and it came from the Zelleys."

Her picture wasn't of the plain Gothic-back chair, now unlocated, that Woodhouse published as the sixth sample, but of a carved rococo one. While I mulled this over, she told why she wasn't in love with the Princeton Museum's chair anyway. Its lower half, especially the rail and leg carvings, went off in one direction and the form of its back in

*For the Earl of Dumphries Chippendale also made a bed like Cadwalader's, fit to bear Aphrodite and her consort under a canopy with shells, scrolls, and tasels (1762 *Director*, Plate 39).

Shortly after Marriage by William Hogarth,
from his series *Marriage à la Mode,* 1743
—National Gallery, London

Hogarth has painted into this overblown Palladian interior a suite of two matching card tables and eight side chairs of the kind called back stools, all in the Queen Anne style.

18th-century cartoon: General von Knyphausen buttering bread with his thumb

—Prints Division,
New York Public Library

another. Garvan, along with a very few other furniture critics such as John Kirk and John Gloag, reacts to a chair as an opera fan to a Bizet overture—the curtain had better go up on something more than a mere rude device for human repose. What counted wasn't whether you could lounge back and put your feet up, but whether this utterance had courage. Her word for the Fanshawes was *robust*.

"Well, the Randolph chair at Yale *is* a bomb," I said, thinking to bait her a little. (That one had belonged to her mother-in-law.)

This seemed to amuse her. I asked if she had more or less succeeded to Woodhouse's old job at the museum.

"Oh, I don't know, it was so small then."

"Who in Philadelphia would remember the dealer James Curran?"

"Have you looked for him in the directories? I'm new in Philadelphia—I've only been here about 25 years! Well, what happened in Ireland, just for laughs?"*

I showed her my correspondence and some photos, which go over better than travel reminiscences, and went link by link down the chairs' chain of owners to the 11th Earl of Westmeath. This held Garvan's attention, for no detailed account had yet circulated in America. Had she seen the underside of the splat shoe in chair VIII upstairs? No, they didn't take the shoe off here, although she had looked at the five chairs up at Parke Bernet in 1974. The Philadelphia Museum just didn't have the money for them then.

"What were they covered with at the gallery that day, damask?"

"No, red leather."

"Leather! Or leather cloth? How old did it look, thirty or forty years?"

"Oh, leather *lasts*."

This lighted uncertainly on my stomach, but we passed on. Whether this covering was Charles Hanlon's work or not, I explained that Gopsill's directories bracketed him as *upholsterer* only from 1901 through 1905.

"Couldn't that mean he worked at Wanamaker's at other times?"

"He wasn't *listed* before 1901."

Now she'd stung.

*Beatrice Bronson Garvan is a native New Yorker. Her entry in *Who's Who* shows B.A. Vassar, M.A. Univ. of Pa., married Barton H. Lippincott, divorced 1969, married Anthony N. B. Garvan; treasurer North Pa. Visiting Nurse Assoc., 1958 Vice Chmn. United Fund Drive North Pa., Councillor HSP, Phila. Museum of Art guide 1962-66, curatorial assistant 1966-71, associate curator 1971–.

Did I imagine people had a life-span of five years? Garvan regarded me sympathetically, which is I think what museum curators do when they don't exactly buy all they are being told.

And leather seats! "*13 Mahogany Chairs carved frames & seats, covered in leather cloth.*" Yes, and why in God's name would an adult male of presumably sane mind fly off over the ocean to inquire after chairs without knowing what in hell they looked like? Hadn't the "13" connected at all—mentally, at least—with the XIII marked in the chair now at Williamsburg?

I said to Beatrice Garvan I might as well get out of her hair now, and she strolled with me into the hall to say goodbye. They'd turned out a beautiful show. A truly beautiful show. *How did 13 chairs in Westmeath's mansion square with the Cadwalader inventories? Some might be left in Ireland after all?*

In his comments on the copperplate engravings making up the 1762 and last edition of *The Gentleman & Cabinet-Maker's Director*, Thomas Chippendale notes of Plate 15, the one that seems to have inspired the Fanshawes: "*Three Designs of Chairs with Ribband-Backs. Several Sets have been made, which have given entire Satisfaction. If any of the small Ornaments should be thought superfluous, they may be left out, without spoiling the Design. If the seats are covered with red Morocco, they will have a fine Effect.*"

At least in the great English houses, "The seats of dining chairs were usually covered with red morocco" (John Kenworthy-Browne, *Chippendale and his Contemporaries* [New York: World Publishing Company, 1973]).

So much for the aesthetics of leather seat covers.

Now two more details came unzipped:

Bennett, the valuer from Dublin, in conducting what is called a chattel appraisal, noted: *13 Mahogany Chairs carved frames & seats, covered in leather cloth. . .£26 5/s.* Why did he describe the carving as in the *frames & seats* when the only part of a seat that can be carved *is* its frame? The frame must be something else than the seat rails? Now it came woefully clear that my vocabulary didn't coincide with Herbert Cescinsky's—in England and Ireland a chair's framing includes its back. Another difference lay in the word *Mahogany*; in Bennett's context it nearly always means Georgian. What he wrote, had I troubled to read him, was that here he had thirteen mahogany period chairs of the later 18th century, their seats *and backs* carved, covered in imitation leather. What else would I like, a photograph?

We know from another source that the dining room at Pallas held more than "Five dining room chairs" on July 16, 1908. That morning J. P. Dalton and his colleagues arrived from the Loughrea station, a bit wet. After touring the castle, they repaired to the house. When his Lordship joined them for lunch, the party totaled six: "Having taken a last admiring look at the perfect bawn, the unshaken ramparts and the venerable tower rising proudly above them all we accompanied our host back to the dining room, where luncheon was served." Until the day turned stormy, fourteen guests were expected (*The Annual Excursion—Pallas*).

So about now the whole thing yawed, as if struck by a heavy sea. Suddenly it looked as if nothing would hold and our ship founder. What happened, instead, was that after a sickening pause the boom and sail swung over our head, catching the wind from the other side, and everything on that side came sliding and rattling to the other. Not very seamanlike, but we were lucky to be afloat.

If the five banquet chairs Nancy Connell carried home to Leixlip in 1934 fitted Bennett's description, as we now knew they did, where at Pallas could they come from? The only source in the inventory was this large set, the thirteen. (Although Westmeath, as already explored, may well have got the five in such a place as London after the valuation—after 1913.) Would the auctioneer, Battersby, break the larger set into two or three lots? To get the bidding going, an auctioneer would break his mother into two or three lots. Later Sotheby Parke Bernet knocked down the Fanshawe set in just this way.

"THE ANTIQUE AND MODERN FURNITURE OF THE MANSION" was sold on June 19 and 20, but we have no record of the second day's furniture.

Dr. Charles might fit Bridget Mary into his master bedroom very nicely, and perhaps five chairs as well. *But thirteen*? In the old photos and *Inquirer* drawings of the South Fourth Street front hall, parlor, and dining room, where are they? In Davis & Harvey's catalogue, where are they?

After going to see Captain John's art and furniture, I dropped him a note asking if I might use photographs of it and venturing that while the evidence putting the Fanshawes in the old Second Street house looked pretty solid, had he come across any evidence of their ever having stood in the South Fourth or Locust Street houses? He generously said yes to our reproductions, refusing payment, but to the last point he didn't reply. The family still runs an office, Cadwalader Estates, at 2024 Delancey Place, which holds records we haven't seen.

Now we might as well run Garvan's comment on the Gopsill's *City Directory* entries up the mast and see how it flapped.

Suppose Charles Hanlon worked at Wanamaker's before setting up as an independent upholsterer perhaps on call to the store? As noted earlier, all Wanamaker's could tell me was that he never got a pension there. He might very well have been doing his thing on a set of thirteen chairs in 1897, and the restored pieces then put on sale in the antiques gallery of the City Hall Square store. Its stock consisted largely of English imports, for which the Fanshawes could certainly pass. The chairs are rather a knockout, especially after Hanlon has brass-nailed fake red leather to the seats! And his pride in the lineup of ancient chairs refreshed by his efforts has not been misplaced, for who should travel there from the British Embassy and purchase them but a Duke or a Lord (*a young prince*?), and carry them back to his castle in Galway? We haven't found the Nugents' "American connections" of which the Major wrote, but turn-of-the-century Washington must have been no place to get stuck over a summer holiday, and Westmeath was in America for over two years.

It's quite idle to say that any number of chairs make an unhandy and expensive parcel to ship overseas when the fact is that somebody did ship them.

Where could Wanamaker's have got them around 1897? We don't know, though it looks nearly certain that furniture wasn't sold out of the South Fourth or Locust Street houses just before 1900. They may have been spilled by the family earlier, even as much as a century earlier. In this case, a piece was still missing, some names we haven't yet heard. Rather a chilling shower on the prospect that Dr. Charles was our shipper and Bridget Mary the vendor—yet this first solution could not be ruled out, for it fits the puzzle as well as the second. Some chairs of the set got left unaccounted for either way. Would I like them here or in Ireland?

So I came back from Philadelphia with two solutions in place of one. Was this twice as good?

Something else surprised me—the Dietrich table. Its popping up this way (a twin to the unique?) was like confronting two Greta Garbos. Bea

Garvan catalogued its provenance as Dietrich Corporation–Lyon–Cadwalader. Assuming this right, the links between Cadwalader and Lyon are still unknown.

In studying the carving, Garvan first spotted differences in style between the card tables and chairs. She was right, too, that the table paws have longer toes and nails that grasp obvious ball forms. She suggested that under Randolph's direction Hercules Courtenay carved the tables and John Pollard the chairs. Now I felt obliged to go a step farther and find the tables not only passed through the hands of a different carver but came from the shop of a different maker as well—Thomas Affleck.

Why? Is this complication just what we need? Whether we need it or not, Affleck made both card tables because he says he did:

Mr John Cadwalader

To Thos Affleck Dr

1771
Jan 2 *To 2 Commode Card Tables @ £5*................................ *10—*

For a time I imagined this line charged for the hairy-paw table that passed from Anne Cadwalader's heir to Winterthur and for a mate to it presumably lost. The trouble here was the word *Commode.* It can't mean a table with drawer, for a few lines above Affleck enters £16 *"To 2 Mahogany Commode Sophias for the Recesses @ 8."* Sofas with drawers? No, to Affleck *Commode* means curved in a certain way, and this is how Hummel reads him: "*Commode* referred to a swelled, or serpentine, front."* The Anne Cadwalader (Winterthur) table, on the other hand, is shaped like a shoe box.

In April 1786 only three card tables stood in the house—one in each of the three parlors—and the General had paid Affleck for two of them. Their carver, then, was James Reynolds or Bernard & Jugiez—again because Affleck says so:

To Mr Reynold's Bill for Carving the Above	*£37*
To Barnard & Jugies Ditto for Ditto	*£24.4*
	£61.4

(Total for carving 20 pieces, including a *harpsicord Frame.)*

*Charles F. Hummel, *A Winterthur Guide to American Chippendale Furniture* (New York: Crown, 1976),p. 79.

Cadwalader pier glass
—Courtesy, The Henry Francis du Pont Winterthur Museum

Card table
—Courtesy, The Henry Francis du Pont Winterthur Museum
Origin Philadelphia, c. 1770. Mahogany, white oak, and yellow pine. 28⅜″ H x 32″ L x 15½″ W (closed). Inherited in 1875 together with the Cadwalader pier glass by Mrs. Henry J. Rowland (Anne Cadwalader) from her uncle William Cadwalader, who was one of General John's grandsons.

The appearance of the Dietrich table not only suggests this attribution, but if we accept—as Downs and Wainright have—the origin of Anne Cadwalader's table in Second Street, it becomes possible to know Dietrich's had existed even before it surfaced in Lyon's stock at Millbrook. When I got down under it at the museum, its drawer was missing, but the drawer runners were still there. The center cabochon teases us by pointing to our left to greet its opposite number in Captain John's table, which points right.

A chronology for this whole suite, which may have included Affleck's sofas and some of his pole (or fire) screens as well, emerges corresponding to the dates of the bills and portraits, although the particulars certainly involve guesswork, too. Our guess, then, is that Cadwalader owned the marble slabs as well as the Fanshawe chairs by the end of 1769, and that late the next year he had Affleck make the pair of serpentine card tables to match the chairs. Randolph and Courtenay possibly found it inconvenient to produce the tables based on their own chair design because in the fall of 1770 they were both up to their chins carving the mahogany paneling in the parlors.

What we think we see in these pieces is a fantastic array of rocaille carving based on the sample chairs. To know that the samples in turn drew from an early Georgian design source flowing around as well as through Chippendale's drawings, we've only to look at the photo here of the Fruiterers Company master's chair c. 1740 now in the Lady Lever Art Gallery, Port Sunlight, Cheshire. Our piece closest in detail, and probably time, to the master's chair is the sample wing chair. Besides the help the samples' designer got from the *Director,* he had patterns, engravings, or perhaps just the memory of something like this in his kit.

Back in New York the next morning, I loitered by the lions on the steps of the 42nd Street Library, smoking a cigarette and waiting for the doors to open. A surprising thing was that when they did open, hardly anybody got up. Here, too, the Bicentennial had just crested. It was a lovely July day, Fifth Avenue still decked with flags.

Admission to the NYPL's Manuscript Division is by card, which you get by filling out other cards. As with the Metropolitan Museum's furniture conservation shop, those outside are locked out and those inside are locked in. The research librarian knew, as soon as I asked, what account book to bring; as old ledgers go, this one had turned hot.

Its pages are not written in Benjamin Randolph's hand and nowhere hold his name. The book was evidently kept by his clerk, and over the

Master's chair, Fruiterers Company, c. 1740

—Lady Lever Art Gallery, Port Sunlight, Cheshire

The hairy-paw feet, leaf sprays, and cross-hatched ground in the crestrail of this early Georgian guild chair all predict details carved later in the Philadelphia samples.

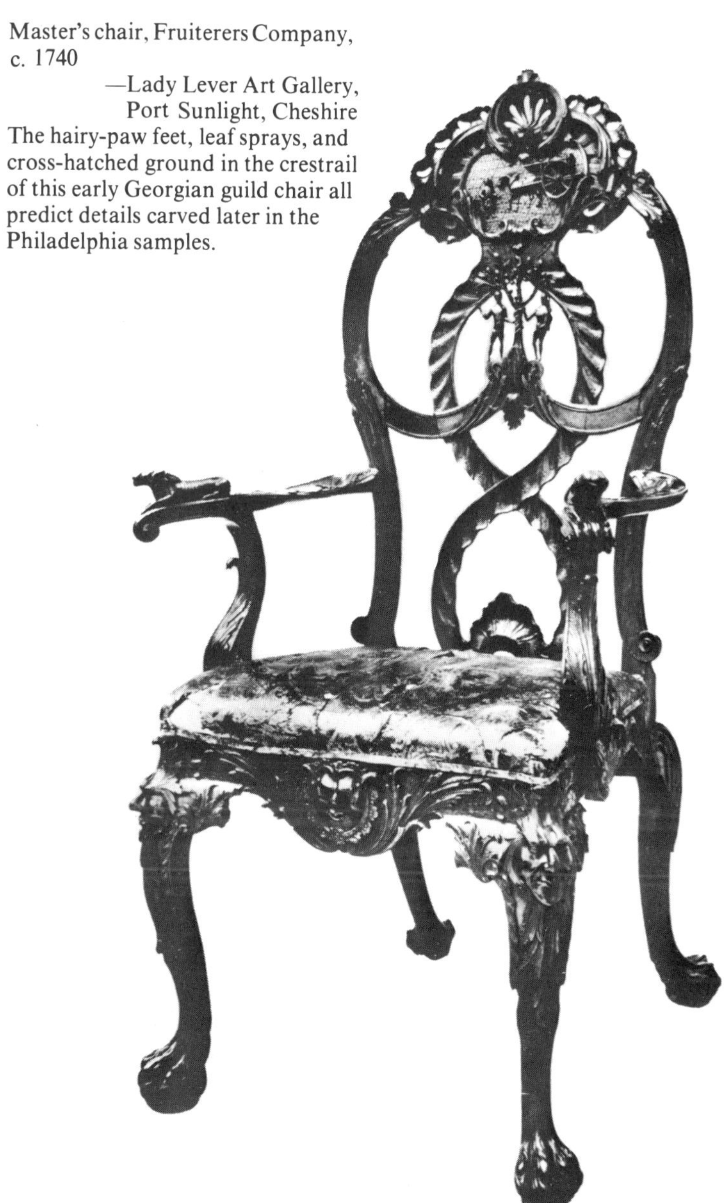

years by more than one. The old gang's names popped up right away—Plunket Fleeson, for one, worked his tail off on the output of Benjamin Randolph's *Shop*. On October 1, 1768, a week after Cadwalader married and the year after Randolph moved to the Sign of the Golden Eagle, we read *To John Cadwallader 125.17.1.* This is entered under the heading *Real Estate,* but as Cadwalader's name here appears in a column of others charged trifling sums of well under £5, we wonder how it could be real estate. Might this be for lodging?* The number of transactions in 1768–69 is astonishing. The acounts are laid on a weird and archaic framework of double-entry bookkeeping, and it's going to take a better accountant than I am to unravel all B.R. was into. In understanding the following entries, all suggestive in one way or another, it usually helps (but not always) to read *By* as *From* and *To* as *For. Adventure* means *venture.*

SAW MILL

Octo. 15, 1768	*By Adventure to London*	*£2.15.10*
	By Adven to ye Bay of Honduras	*18.12*
	Voyage to Jamaica of Ship Diana Jn. Clarke Comm.	*110.12*

DR THOMAS NEVIL†

Octo. 1768	*To John & Lambt Cadwallader*	*7.8.9*
1769	*To Sloop Betsy*	[several payments]
Apr. 11, 1769	*Adventure to London ye Ship Penn's Pacquet*	*Sundry Accompts 1040.4.3¾*

GEN GEORGE WASHINGTON

June 20, 1775	*To Sundrys*	*By Cash in full 17—9*

THOMAS JEFFREISON ESQ.

July 22, 1775	*To Expences*	*10.3.6*

BRIG RECOVERY

Novem. 12, 1778	*To Cash &c.*	*21,602.14.7½*

*At the left edge the trade card shows a sign on Randolph's housefront, *The New Boardabo.* This word has sunk from our language, succeeded by "boarding house."

†In setting out to remodel the Second Street house the following summer, Thomas Nevell was Cadwalader's master carpenter.

SCHOONER HUMMING BIRD

Aug. 11, 1779 To Cash *2,793.14.5*

BRIG ARGO FITTED OUT AS A PRIVATEER

Novem & Decem 1779 [sum of about £100,000 unclear]

Our idea of Ben Randolph the carpenter being run out of his trade in 1778 by the rude British has now been jostled a bit. His ships came in like Rhett Butler's, starting with the *Recovery* on November 12 of that year and possibly, though we doubt it, ending with a haul from the armed brig *Argo* that had even his bookkeeper's hand shaking! These amounts reflect, too, the runaway inflation of paper money. But truly, who would rise to censure the Father of his Country for trying to turn a buck on his expense account?

After the war, when B.R. felt he had grounds on which to rest his occupation as "gentleman," we see no more *Shop* accounts. For 1785 through 1787 the ledger shows more modest receipts from Speedwell Works totaling £2,988. Having bought out his brother Daniel's interest in the sawmill in 1778, Randolph established an iron forge there. We could imagine now that the sample chairs did not look out of place in his house. By the time Randolph died in 1791, the samples must have stood as exemplars of his early striving and triumphs in the rococo style, and maybe as mementos of his friends Courtenay and Pollard, both already gone. That is what they seem to be today.

Things aren't always as they seem, however, and now, having phoned William Stahl's office at the auction gallery earlier, I got on a Madison Avenue bus and went uptown to see him. Was Garvan's recollection of the leather seats exact? The appraiser at Pallas called them *leather cloth.*

Bill Stahl was raised on and probably under antiques by his mother, a dealer in Waverly, Pennsylvania, near Scranton. He took a bachelor's degree in art history at Trinity College, Hartford, in June 1974 and a month later found himself understudying Ronald De Silva at SPB New York. At college he was next to, and often working in, one of New England's great furniture collections, Wallace Nutting's, given to the Wadsworth Atheneum by J. P. Morgan, Jr. Just before graduating, Stahl wrote SPB asking for a job, and it was the only such letter he had to write. That summer he made the now well-known drive down the New Jersey Turnpike with De Silva, carrying the two Fanshawes in back.

After the auction in November his boss moved on, and Stahl, then 23, became one of the two experts running the Americana department. The other, Nancy Druckman, was also in her twenties.

Even the cops in this town were starting to look like schoolboys!

The bus struggled past a new storefront in the upper 70s, its sign lettered gold on black: *Ronald A. De Silva Inc. American Furniture & Decorations.* For a moment the sign looked as inscrutable as the poems of Chairman Mao.

My God, had I chased these crazy mothers for eighteen months?

What had we caught of value but the people mirrored in them? The material nailed to the seat rails didn't concern me right then; I was thinking of Randolph. The truth of his as well as the Cadwaladers' links to the chairs remained puzzling and opaque, as if seen through gauze, still resisting being sucked from the grave. This had to do with the intractability of antiques or, as Dryden says, of the past itself. To add a few faces to the circle had been nice, but *what if?* What if the premises the Randolph samples rested on proved defective? What if other indicators lied or got misread? Then we had only a bunch of fancy chairs, and among them the Fanshawes, lost again somewhere off Chestnut Street. In which case I'd not only saved these bits and pieces, but jumbled some—to be reassembled later on by a perhaps grateful posterity?

The auction house now went through the motions of trying to protect Stahl from chance callers with bundles, as the girl at the desk said rather sharply, "Do you have an appointment?" Stahl came out, personable and direct. He led me into a small cockpit of a room that held metal chairs and a table on which I laid my parcel of catalogues and notes—its bare surface spoke of the steel one in a vet's office on which many a faithful pet has made his farewell.

We talked over the numbering of the chairs. Apparently the "II" in Winterthur's led to its being called the second sample, although the joiner struck this numeral to show its sequence in the complete Fanshawe set. I saw no problem in its being withdrawn at random for a floor model, a keepsake, or a status symbol to the trade—what counted was its origin in Randolph's shop.

Stahl glanced at the Philadelphia Museum's catalogue photo of chair VIII, now silk-covered.

"Did this have leather on it when you first saw it?"

"Not real leather—oh, an orange red leatherette, like Naugahyde. . . ."

Naugahyde, a word from the dawn of synthetics! A fabric cheaper than red Morocco, to be preferred if you had to cover thirteen seats.

"Might that stuff be sixty years old, seventy?"

"When did they start making it? Sack may have kept samples—they did some work on them down there."

Stahl sat back, agreeably recalling the game of the hairy-paw chairs and his first big play in which he was privileged to run interference for De Silva. At Winterthur they microanalyzed small wedges cut from the glueblocks. But the clock in the stadium moves on.

"I have another piece here right now, a great one, from Paris."

"A desk?"

"A blockfront secretary."

Another American stray, lost on the Continent! A Madison Avenue dealer visiting a friend in Paris first saw the Queen Anne secretary standing in his apartment there. A miniature fitted in it bore John Smibert's signature on the back, and there were other interesting things inside. But no, I didn't have $60,000 just then or, in fact, any lunch.

After going over the Irish particulars of the Fanshawes for a few minutes, I got up and we walked toward the elevator.

"Who owned them in Ireland isn't the problem any more," I said. "The problem is right here on this side, in Philadelphia. When you get to sailing them over the ocean, you can go more than one way. With the Cadwalader family there are ramifications."

"It may never be known," Stahl said cheerfully.

Appendix 1

THE ANNUAL EXCURSION, 1908*
by J. P. Dalton

PALLAS

The Annual Excursion of the Society took place on the 16th July. The weather, unhappily, proved most unfavourable. The appointed morning broke on a regular tempest of rain and wind; and, the downpour not desisting as the hours advanced, the most ardent archaeologist might well have been excused for hesitating to venture from home. Fourteen members were to have joined in the day's proceedings, but only four of the number assembled on the platform of the Railway Station at Loughrea on the arrival of the 11 o'clock train. The little party consisted of Miss M. Redington, Dr. Costello, Mr. Trench (who was accompanied by Mr. Stockley of Cork) and Mr. Dalton. On taking counsel together they were disposed at first to relinquish the journey; but as conveyances were in attendance and all arrangements completed, it was finally decided to go through with the programme. Their perseverance was rewarded, in some measure, by a temporary cessation of the rain; but throughout the day the atmosphere continued moist and forbidding, and the excursionists had to defend themselves against its rigours as best they could by means of waterproofs and umbrellas.

The castle which Richard de Burgo, son of Fitzadelm, erected at Loughrea in 1236 is not now to be seen, and its exact site cannot be identified. A small square tower still standing near the gate of the new

*Excerpted from *Journal of the Galway Archaeological & Historical Society*, Vol. V (1907-8), pp. 213-24.

Cathedral grounds formed, doubtless, part of its outworks; but this did not call for any lengthened inspection. The day was too inclement for attempting even a hurried survey of the crannogs on the adjoining lake; and it was thought advisable to omit minor items, and to drive direct to Pallas, one of the chief objects of the day's sightseeing. The journey, which measures some 10 or 11 miles, was made at a good pace. The castle of Leitrim, still looking strong and well-preserved, lay within a field of the road, but it was passed without halting; and about one o'clock the horses drew up in front of the Earl of Westmeath's fine mansion of Pallas.

Lord Westmeath had come home specially to meet the party, and he placed us under great obligations by his courteous attentions during the day. He took us through the principal rooms and showed us the many objects of interest preserved in the modern residence. The hall proved to be a very special attraction. Lined with paintings and works of art it is, in truth, a miniature picture-gallery. Over the chimney-piece is a large-size portrait of the first Lord Riverston who, as is well know, was James the Second's Chief Justice of the King's Bench in Ireland. To the right and left of this picture hang portraits of the monarch himself—James II.—and of his queen, Mary of Modena. These three paintings are all by Sir Peter Lely; and, having regard to the distinction of the artist and the historic importance of the personages they represent, their value must now be very considerable. On the wall facing the door are several other portraits of members of the Nugent family—the ancestors of the present Earl—all of which were examined under his Lordship's guidance.

The ancient castle stands a little to the right of the modern residence. The fine old keep is visible from the lawn, but the view of the ramparts is cut off by intervening buildings. The castle occupies a central and commanding position on the extensive plain that was once the rich lordship of Clanrickarde; but, hidden away now by a well-wooded demesne, the square keep is no longer a conspicuous object from the surrounding country. In his *Visitation of the Seats and Arms of Noblemen and Gentlemen of Great Britain and Ireland,* (1855) the late Sir J. Bernard Burke, referring to Pallas, wrote: "the castle whose architecture dates of the fourteenth century, is still as habitable as when the last stone was placed on the rampart." The statement may be made with even more propriety now than when it was written, for the present Earl takes a special pride in this splendid monument of mediaeval times. Since he inherited the estates he has devoted much care to the renovation of the place; castle and appurtenances are kept with scrupulous taste, and the strictest regard is paid to the preservation of all the primitive features. Unlike the great majority of the Norman castles of the country, which have been allowed everywhere to go to ruin—which in many cases have disappeared altogether—the old fortress of Pallas has, indeed, been singularly fortunate in its owners.

In the work from which I have already quoted, Sir J. Bernard Burke gives a general description of the castle, and I cannot do better than draw again from the same competent source. His sketch still exactly applies. He writes:

> "The keep consists of a lofty square tower. The entrance passes under a pointed arch, and leads through the hall, which has on the right a recess for warders, and a stone spiral staircase on the left, into a capacious guardroom. The vaulted stone ceiling of this nook-like hall is perforated for the purpose of hurling stone, boiling water, or lead on any enemy who might succeed in forcing the massy door, and who would then find himself exposed to a cross fire, or the cross stabs of lance or sword, thrusting from the lateral recesses of the warders' hold and the staircase opposite, together with the whole force of the garrison, not employed on the battlement, collected in the guardroom directly facing the low and narrow entrance. The largest windows, as usual, are on the topmost story, which was the grand reception hall, strongly contrasting with the apartments below, lighted only by narrow loop-holes. The roof is surrounded by a plain parapet, while the walls of the rampart enclosure are dentellated into that picturesque triple-graded battlement generally met with in Ireland. The battlement, being less than half the width of the thick wall, thus left a stage or landing running all round and communicating with the ground by several flights of steps, on which stood the men-at-arms and retainers, when arrayed against a besieging force."

. . . There came a time in the later years of occupancy of these grim old castles when their owners, relieved in some measure of the constant fear of external attack, grew tired of being confined within their dungeon-like walls and abandoned them, at least in times of peace, for more open, but less imposing, edifices. Pallas had a residence of this kind, which appears to have remained intact until comparatively recent years. Sir B. Burke found it there in 1855, and described it as "that wide-windowed mansion, machicolated however over the doorway, and strong against surprise." The building is no longer there; but the place where it stood, close beside the keep, is clearly shown by the tracings which its rear elevation impressed on the rampart wall. It was taken down some years after the date of Sir B. Burke's visit, the stones being used as building material for extensions and improvements of the present house. Though not demolished wantonly, or for any unworthy purpose, as so many ancient structures have been, one cannot help regretting that the indulgent care devoted to the original tower was not extended to its later annexe, and that this representative specimen of the style of housing used by the Irish gentry in the transition period between mediaeval and modern times has not been preserved.

. . . Having taken a last admiring look at the perfect bawn, the unshaken ramparts and the venerable tower rising proudly above them all we accompanied our host back to the dining room, where luncheon was served. As we entered again among the portraits that adorn the hall the faces this time, after the hour thus spent, seemed to draw us towards them with a nearness of personal interest which they did not possess before; for we felt that here we were looking at the actors who gave life and meaning to the stage whose disused scenery we had been so closely examining. . . . The old castle of Pallas has outlived the memories that would have given depth and fulness to its human appeal. But who can doubt that hidden away in its historic background lie the materials of many a stirring tale? . . .

Pallas is in the barony of Leitrim, which is part of the ancient Moenmagh, the territory of the O'Naghtens and the O'Mullallys. Under date 1237 the Four Masters made the following significant entry: "The English Barons of Ireland having settled in Connaught commenced building castles there." The most ambitious and active of these barons was Richard, the son of William Fitzadelm and cousin of Hubert De Burgh, the Justiciar of Henry III. Several castles were built before the date given, and among others Richard himself had built the castle of Dunbo na Gaillve, or Galway, in 1231. The significance of the entry in The Four Masters does not consist in fixing the date of the first building of Norman castles, for it has so much meaning, but in its determining the time when the Norman settlers commenced to establish themselves securely and to take effective possession of the land. "All the land of Connaught," with the exception of five cantreds near Athlone, had been granted to De Burgo, on the forfeiture of King Oethos (Hugh) O'Connor, by a royal charter dated 21st May 1227. Royal charters, however, were of no avail until the power of the native chiefs was broken; but this consummation was being hastened by the fratricidal strife of the family which, from early Milesian times, had given kings to the province. . . .

The date when Pallas was built cannot now be ascertained, nor is there any record of the builder's name; but that it was built by the De Burgos there cannot, I think, be a particle of doubt. . . . All the evidences, architectural and other, point to Pallas having been built sometime in the 14th century as a residence for one of the principal men of the De Burgo clan, not improbably for a younger son of the MacWilliam of the day [i.e., a MacWilliam Uachtar later married into the De Burgo clan] . . . . It is known that the owner of the castle in 1574 was Jonyck FitzThomas Burke. . . .

The lands needed for the "Settlement of Connaught" were, as is well known, obtained by extensive forfeitures of the estates of gentlemen like . . . Thomas Burke who had sided with Charles I. against his rebellious parliament. The history of these transactions, so far as they relate to Pallas, is well summarised by Sir B. Burke in a passage which I transcribe in full:-

> "When the rebellion of 1641, which was decided to have commenced on the 23rd October in that year, broke out, all the lands in the neighborhood of Pallas were forfeited, and they were afterwards 'appointed' to the Earl of Westmeath by the Usurpers' Commissioners sitting at Loughreagh, in 'part satisfaction of his former estate, and upon his transplantation into Connaught,' which was acted upon and effected by decree of the Commissioners sitting at Athlone. The Earl of Westmeath, returning on the restoration of the royal family to the ancient family domains in that county, held since the time of Henry II., conferred Pallas, and the extensive Galway estates, on his second son, the Hon. Thomas Nugent, afterwards created Lord Riverston, and they were confirmed to him by King Charles II., by letters enrolled on the patent roll (23rd Feb., 29 Charles II.) which patent, embellished with a miniature portrait of that monarch, beautifully painted in oil colours, is still preserved with the patent creating the peerage of Riverston, the patents of Lord Chief Justice, and numerous other interesting documents in the muniment chests at Pallas."

This brings us to the exciting period of the Revolution when the Nugents, like most of the old Celtic and Norman families, attached themselves devotedly to the fortunes of James. In camp and council members of the family held high positions. Colonel The Hon. William Nugent, son of Richard the second Earl of Westmeath, specially distinguished himself in the military operations of 1689. His elder brother, The Hon. Thomas Nugent, who was then the owner of Pallas, had been bred to the law and had been advanced by James to the position of Chief Justice of the King's Bench in Ireland. On the 3rd April, 1689, he was created Baron Riverston. He figures prominently in all the histories of the period, and will be particularly remembered by readers of Macaulay and of Sheridan Lefanu's historical novel "Sir Torlough O'Brien." Assured of the highest rank in James's Government the promise of his career was blighted by the overthrow of that unhappy monarch, and after the capitulation of Limerick he returned to an uneventful life in Pallas, where he died in 1715.

The annals of the Nugent family in the eighteenth century exhibit the usual succession of attainders, litigations, designs of "discoverers," and other such products of this black period. Notwithstanding many adverse influences the family succeeded in retaining possession of the castle and of a good portion of the estates. But the title, though conferred seven days before the declaration of the rebellion, and acknowledged by the Baron De Ginkell in a letter of safe conduct for Lord Riverston and his family "given at the camp before Limerick, this 5th October, 1691," was disallowed by William's Government. Nevertheless the owners of Pallas continued to be recognised by general courtesy as Lords Riverston down to the middle of the 19th century. Over the door of the National School of Tynagh, which stands just outside the demesne walls, is a cut stone bearing the inscription: "Built by Lord Riverston in 1845." The Lord Riverston of that time (William Thomas Nugent) died on the 6th September, 1851, and was succeeded by his son Anthony Francis, the grandfather of the present Earl. This gentleman finally dropped the title of Riverston; but the senior branch of the Nugent family having become extinct the older and higher title of Earl of Westmeath came to him subsequently by legal inheritance. He was succeeded by William the tenth Earl, who died on the 31st May, 1883, leaving the title and estates to his son, the present Earl. In Earl William's time additions were built to the new residence and other extensive improvements were made at Pallas.

Luncheon over, the afternoon was already well advanced, and it became necessary to make an immediate start for Kilnalahan, the next stage in our archaeological tour. The Earl of Westmeath had placed us under many obligations during the day, and he now kindly accompanied us most of the way. . . .

Appendix 2

CHARLES WILLSON PEALE AND JOHN CADWALADER

The lives of these two intertwine for a little.

Peale was born at Chestertown, not far from Shrewsbury plantation on the Eastern Shore of Maryland in 1741, just a year before Cadwalader. His father, a school teacher, died nine years later, and his mother apprenticed Peale at 13 to a saddler. By the time he got through his middle twenties Peale himself had set up and failed as a saddler, married an Annapolis girl, Rachel Brewer, and had a go at clockmaking, silversmithing, and local politics. He had something like Franklin's energy, versatility, and spirit, if not his way with money. On February 9, 1764, he began running an ad in the *Maryland Gazette*:

> CHARLES WILSON PEALE
>
> *At his Shop* in Church-Street, ANNAPOLIS MAKES, Cleans and Repairs CLOCKS, and Cleans and Mends WATCHES, in the best, neatest and cheapest Manner, and with the greatest Expedition. Any Gentleman who shall be pleas'd to Employ him, may depend on being faithfully served, by
>
> *Their humble Servant,*
> CHARLES WILSON PEALE
>
> N.B. He likewise carries on the SADDLERS Business in all it's Branches as heretofore.

Until his creditors drove him out, Peale also painted signs there. He tried his hand too at limning, having been introduced to its mysteries by John Hesselius. Then, four writs having been served on him, he left his pregnant wife for a time and fled by sea to Boston. Fancying the extra *l* in Willson, Peale called the new baby James Willson. He named five of his later sons, born when he was well into art, Raphaelle, Rembrandt, Titian, Rubens, and Vandyke.

In 1766, as Peale cheerfully held his creditors at bay, some of the Annapolis gentry raised enough money by subscription to send him to England. His sponsors included John Beal Bordley, who soon purchased lands for a plantation next to the Lloyds' in Talbot County. Another donor was Thomas Ringgold. They sent him off to London with a rather cool letter addressed by the barrister Charles Carroll to his agent over there:

> The Bearer hereof Charles Wilson Peale a young man of this Town has a turn for Limning and some other Branches of Painting. He has Likewise Pretensions to an Interest in Oxfordshire. As his Circumstances are but Low I am willing to advance twenty or twenty five Guineas to Enable him to take a Trip to England to see what he can make of his Pretensions and to get some further Insight into the Profession. I therefore desire that you will at all times as he shall want it Let him have in the whole to the amount of the above sum and Charge the Same to my Account. If it lays in your way and you can Recommend him to the Employ of or Get Him Introduced to any of the Profession it may be of Service to him and I shall be obliged to you as I have no other motive to what I advance but to give him an opportunity of Improving himself That he may be better able to Support himself and Family. I hope he will behave with Diligence and Frugality.*

In London Benjamin West took him in and taught him. Peale's hope of inheriting a manor house in Oxfordshire came to nothing, but he returned from West's painting room two years later with a command of portraiture probably then surpassed in America only by John Singleton Copley's. It was Copley in Boston who had given the young runaway a kind word and a glimpse of what a portrait might be. Now at Annapolis

*Carroll's 1766 letter as well as much other manuscript material now in the American Philosophical Society, Philadelphia, has been collected by Charles Coleman Sellers, a Peale descendant, in *Charles Willson Peale* (New York: Scribner, 1969). To Sellers's definitive biography I owe a good deal of the information here.

and Philadelphia there was room at the top. In the next few years, painting each day until the light failed, Peale got there.

His studio was fitted out in the family household on North Street, Annapolis. It presently happened that Bordley's half-brother in England, Edmund Jennings, wanted a portrait of John Dickinson, whose mother was Dr. Thomas Cadwalader's sister.* Dickinson became an American resistance leader with his 1768 publication of *Letters from a Farmer in Pennsylvania to the Inhabitants of the British Colonies.* In the spring or early summer of 1770 Peale packed his colors and traveled with his wife and baby girl to Philadelphia to execute the commission. There he also found Cadwaladers to be painted.

From both Dickinson and John Cadwalader, he got encouragement in the form of more work than he could handle. Although Peale's diaries cover over half a century, the one for 1770 has been lost, so we'll probably never know where he lodged and set up his easel that summer. Before September 7 he went back to Maryland, leaving some projects undone, for on that date he wrote to John Cadwalader:

> Dear Sir
>
> I have sent a Case for Mrs Cadwalader's Picture by the post.
>
> Mr Bordly has expected me over to the Island some time, and I intend to paint your landscapes there, if I can find Views that will look well in painting. I can there amuse Mr Bordly with a part of the art which he is exceedingly fond of, and I shall be out of the way of being importuned about my unfinished portraits.
>
> I am not certain that I shall not See Philadelphia this Winter for I have a great desire to Settle there, and at liasure Times be a Visitor in Maryland, to do the Business I have here.
>
> I hope Mr Dickinson approves of the finishing of his Portrait, and does excuse my hasty leave of your City. I ought to have portrayed Mr Dickinson's aunt before I returned, but my affairs were in so critical a situation that I could not do as I would. I promise to do this piece the first opportunity.
>
> Mrs Peale and little Nelly are well. Mrs Peale beggs with me that our respects may be acceptable to Mrs Cadwalader.
>
> I am Dear Sir, your much obliged very Humble Servant
>
> Charles Peale

*A partial set of John Dickinson's Chippendale chairs is now lodged in the HSP. These two chairs look only a little less grand than the Fanshawes. They are marked IIII and VIIII, have heavy seat rails mortised through the back legs, some original quarter-round blocks in their frames, slip seats, and claw-and-ball front feet. The splats are pierced but not carved.

The "Case" must have been for his miniature of Betsy Cadwalader. The "Island" was Wye, in Talbot County, Maryland, where Peale's old schoolmate John Beal Bordley had just settled near the Lloyd plantation. Cadwalader asked for landscapes of the countryside to hang in Second Street, but Peale never got around to doing them. Instead the fall went by as he executed a large portrait of Bordley laden with patriotic symbols, rather a heavyhanded mishmash, as his 1768 mezzotint of William Pitt had been. Apparently his promise to do "Mr Dickinson's aunt" at the first opportunity goes to an aunt other than Mrs. Thomas (Hannah Lambert) Cadwalader, whose portrait as well as her husband's and Lambert's he'd just finished. (Dickinson had two other aunts on his mother's side. Had John Cadwalader's mother been the still unpainted lady, the artist likely would have said so.) Finally, the compliments from Rachel Peale to Betsy Cadwalader show that the Peales had been warmly received. His new patrons had opened the door to Philadelphia and were urging him in.

Peale spent parts of each year there, by July 1772 finishing the *John Cadwalader Family*. On July 29 of that year he wrote Bordley:

> I am once more making a Tryal how far the Arts will be favoured in the City. I have now on hand . . . one composition of Mr John Cadwaleder Lady & Child in half length Sise, which is greatly admired. . . . I have some prospect of the Quakers incouragement for I find that none of the Painters heretofore have pleased in Likeness—whether I can a little time will show.

But the signature *"C W Peale pinxt 1771"* has lately been reported at the lower left of the canvas. I couldn't see it. Dorinda Evans, who catalogued this painting for the 1976 Philadelphia Museum's Bicentennial show, cites Sellers in noting that Peale put the earliest possible dates on his pictures to remind his patrons it was time to pay up. Even so, in view of the letter to Bordley, Evans hesitates to accept the 1771 date, and on another account we're inclined to reject it entirely. In 1771 Anne Cadwalader (later Mrs. Robert T. Kemble) scarcely could have been as big as the child on the table, having been born that fall. The General bought her cradle, auctioned in 1904 as his own, from William Robinson on December 28, 1771, for £3. The second baby, Elizabeth, was born in 1774.

At any rate Peale eventually got £25.4 for the portrait, though Evans has found that he still listed it in 1775 with others not yet fully paid for.

Evidently the carver collected first, since on March 22, 1774, the General's secretary, William Gouge, paid Hercules Courtenay £28 for two picture frames. These had the family portrait and sister Martha Cadwalader's mounted in them, being the frames Courtenay copied from the three furnished by Reynolds in 1770. The set of five Peales was now complete.

In June 1776 the artist finally loaded his family retinue of ten and wordly goods into wagons and set them down in a rented house on Arch Street. There he reestablished his studio. John Adams, who seems to have gotten into every house and met everyone in Philadelphia, came to call and appraised Peale:

> Yesterday Morning I took a Walk, into Arch Street, to see Mr Peele's Painters Room. Peele is from Maryland, a tender, soft, affectionate Creature. . . . He shewed me a large Picture containing a Group of Figures, which upon Inquiry I found were his Family. His Mother, and his Wifes Mother, himself and his Wife, his Brothers and sisters, and his Children, Sons and Daughters all young. There was a pleasant, a happy Chearfulness in their Countenances, and a Familiarity in their Airs towards each other. . . .* He shewed me one moving Picture. His Wife, all bathed in Tears, with a Child about six months old, laid out, upon her Lap.† This Picture struck me prodigiously. . . . He shewed me too a great Number of Miniature Pictures, among the rest Mr Hancock and his Lady—Mr. Smith, of S.C. whom you saw the other day in Boston—Mr. Custis, and many others. . . . He shewed me, likewise, Draughts, or rather Sketches of Gentlemen's Seats in Virginia, where he has been—Mr. Corbins, Mr. Pages, General Wahingtons &c. . . . He is ingenious. He has Vanity—loves Finery—Wears a sword—gold Lace—speaks French—is capable of Friendship, and strong Family Attachments and natural Affections.
>
> [John to Abigail Adams, Philadelphia, August 21, 1776].

By now the Franklin in Peale had surfaced more than once. He invented with David Rittenhouse a telescopic sight for his rifle that when he fired hit him in the eye. They fitted it with a spring. He constructed his own guitar and sang in French. He joined the City Militia and was elected a Lieutenant. The prospect of beating the King's troops seems to have enthused Peale; in mid-1775 he wrote Benjamin West in London:

**The Peale Family* (1773, completed 1809), New-York Historical Society.

†*Rachel Weeping* (1772, completed 1776), The Barra Foundation, Philadelphia. The baby is Margaret Peale, who died of smallpox in 1772.

> The People here are prepareing for the worst. General Washington has now in pay 16,000 men. One thousand of these are riffle and minite men, Raising in every province. The King of England never had such an army. Here are men who act as common soldiers worth 100,000.

But he'd hardly settled his family on Arch Street when the war news turned bad. In August 1776 Peale's brother and brother-in-law were routed with the Maryland battalions at the Battle of Long Island. A few weeks later, while Washington stood helplessly on the Palisades above the Hudson, his whole garrison in Fort Washington on the Manhattan heights surrendered, including Colonel Lambert Cadwalader.

The remnants of the Continental units on the Jersey shore retreated in some disarray to the Delaware River, losing in their rear one of their generals, Charles Lee, who was captured lodged in an inn. Congress evacuated from Philadelphia and on December 5 Peale was mobilized and ferried up the Delaware, where his city battalion was put under the command of Colonel John Cadwalader.

A month later—maybe the most critical month of all—everything had changed. Washington had turned and stabbed Cornwallis in the tail at Trenton, and while the British rushed reinforcements down to the Delaware, Washington moved on Princeton. Nearly half his army, the Pennsylvania militia and five regiments of Continentals, he entrusted to Cadwalader, whose promotion to brigadier was received on Christmas Eve. Peale commanded a platoon. Just after midnight on January 3, 1777, they were all broken out of camp and formed in column on an icy back road. Peale later wrote in his *Diary:*

> I realy expected a Retreat.
> 3d. At one Oclock in the morning we began to move, and directed our Course through the Woods directly from the River and after some time more northerly. By this I expected we were going to surround the Enemy, but after marching some miles I learnt that we was going a Bye Road. . . . We were marched perty fast. However, the Sun had risen just before we See Prinstown. We proceeded as fast as possible and was within a mile of the Town when we were informed that all was quiet. A short time after, the Battn. just ahead of us began a Exceeding quick Platoon firing and some Cannon. We marched on quick and met some of the Troops retreating in confusion. We continued our march towards the Hill where the firing was, tho' now rather irregularly. I carried my Platoon to the Top of the Hill & fired, tho' very unwillingly, for I thought the Enemy rather too far off, and then retreated, Loading. We Returned to the charge, & fired a 2nd time & Retreated as before. The

3rd time coming up, the Enemy began to Retreat. I must here give the New England troops their due. They were the first who regularly formed. . . . & stood the fire without regarding Balls which whistled their thousand different notes around our heads, and what is very astonishing did little or no harm: none that I know of where we were. Some that had retreated and then advanced through a Wood on our right engaged the Enemy. We lost in all about 12 men. Genl. Mercer was wounded in his Leg and fell into the Enemys Hands when our men was first surprised, and when they in turn was obliged to give way, they stabed him with a Bayonet. We lost, besides, Captn. Shippen of 2 Battn & Lieutenant in the 1st Batn. of Pha. Militia.

We now advanced towards the Town, & halted at about ¼ of a mile distance till the Artilery came up and our men were collected in better order. Amediately on the Artilery firing, a Number that had formed near the College began to disperse, and amediately a Flag was sent, and we huzared Victory.

[Diary, Dec. 4, 1776—Jan. 20, 1777, Henry E. Huntington Library]

What had happened? The Americans coming down a parallel stretch of road had sideswiped just two British regiments, escorted by dragoons and commanded by Lieutenant Colonel Charles Mawhood. Mawhood was then moving to join Cornwallis's main force at Trenton. Until this hour Cornwallis imagined that he had Washington pinned against the Delaware. The outnumbered British broke the first line of Continentals with a bayonet charge, wounding General Mercer. They then drove in the forward units of Cadwalader's militia, so that Washington felt obliged to ride into the Pennsylvanians and rally them. Nobody knew if these fellows could or would fight. For a time the field must have been glutted with confused American units; against overwhelming numbers it was Mawhood who led the "Thin red line." Finally from back in the van the New England regiments and Peale's came up, formed and held, pouring so much shot on Mawhood that he chose to break off the engagement. Apparently he succeeded in regaining the main road by simply charging through the American line. Leaving their artillery pieces on the field, the British ran down the Trenton road. In the town of Princeton a third regiment, which had been left as garrison, was routed by General John Sullivan. These defenders then fell back on Nassau Hall and surrendered.

The exhausted army struggled out of Princeton with its victory and on to Somerset Courthouse and at last to Morristown. On the march Peale bought skins to make moccasins for his men, whose shoes were shot.

They feared that at any moment the British would fall on their rear. Cornwallis tried to catch them but, worrying for the safety of his supply depot at New Brunswick, ended his pursuit. Then he made a fatal error—he retired to wait out the winter in New York. He had scarcely lost the war, but now Washington and even some of the farmers of New Jersey thought they might win it.

The Pennsylvanians soon went home, leaving Washington to try to beg his dwindling effectives into sticking out the winter in their crude huts at Morristown. Peale returned to his Arch Street painting room and to another enthusiasm, Whig politics. Having been appointed to arrest or parole Philadelphia Tories, Captain Peale called on loyalist James Tilghman and invited his choice. Back at Annapolis in 1761 it was Tilghman who invested in young Peale's saddlery and later put the sheriff on him. Tilghman gave his parole, as Lambert Cadwalader had given his to the British.

From 1779, Peale's production of Washington portraits went forward in earnest—their faces look nicer than the Gilbert Stuart portrait on American dollar bills. The artist's construction of gala triumphal arches and his still later invention, as a museum impresario, of a process for stuffing birds and animals (Franklin sent over his dead cat) don't really concern us here. As his life and fame lengthened, Peale seems to have last met John Cadwalader in the arena of bitter local politics. Peale's radical Whigs slowly gained control of Pennsylvania. Through 1779 the propertied conservatives, including Dickinson and the Cadwaladers, resisted—their views didn't exactly coincide with those of the dispossessed and maybe they suffered from rich man's syndrome, fear of being ripped off. The shape of things to come looked volatile. That summer, as John Cadwalader rose on a platform to defend the conservatives, he was howled down by a mob with clubs, to the accompaniment of fifes and drums. To Peale's embarrassment, his commanding officer and old friend had to step down unheard. The rococo fashion in America had already ended.

Appendix 3

HERCULES COURTENAY

Of all the players in the Fanshawe chair puzzle there's none I'd more like to have a few words with than Hercules Courtenay. His claim on our curiosity is summed up in a ledger entry made by a Philadelphia tailor, Joseph Graisbury, on July 16, 1767: "*To Mr. Randolf joyner in Chestnut Street To making your Carver Courteney a barygane Coat 0.16.0*" (HSP, Reed & Forde Papers). That's a bargain coat?

Courtenay can first be found in the record as a signer of the Non-Importation Agreement of 1765. By this or the next year he must have been working for Randolph, since that cabinetmaker's receipt book (Winterthur Museum) shows a payment to one Jacob Chrystler, December 23, 1766, "*on acct of Hercules Corteney.*" A few months later one of Randolph's property transfers is witnessed by Courtenay. Randolph's account book (New York Public Library) shows modest payments to Courtenay and John Pollard in 1768 and a larger amount, £59.74.0, in Courtenay's account in October-November 1769. But by the summer of 1769 Courtenay had moved up from journeyman carver to master of his own shop, for on August 14 he put an ad in the *Pennsylvania Chronicle:*

> Hercules Courtenay, Carver and Gilder, from London, INFORMS his Friends and the Public, that he undertakes all Manner of CARVING and GILDING, in the newest Taste, at his House in Front-Street, between Chestnut and Walnut Streets. N.B. He is determined to be as reasonable as possible in his Charges, and to execute all Commands with the utmost Diligence.

Other notices in the *Pennsylvania Gazette* announce him as lately from London. So in the literature as early as 1925 James J. Bordley

(*Bulletin of the Pennsylvania Museum of Art*) says Courtenay was "A Carver and Gilder from London."

That he carved and gilded the latest in rococo splendor in the Cadwalader parlors there can't be any doubt, and this job he did in collaboration with Randolph. Courtenay's bill to John Cadwalader of September 17, 1770, starts off with *"To 27 Books of Gold laid on Cornice £12.3."* It goes on to itemize charges for carving *rope, Tablet, Freezes, Festoons, Flowers,* and *Leaf Grass,* topped by £8.10 *"To a Tablet the Judgment of Hercule"* (Hercules). This relief was bracketed by festoons over the front parlor fireplace. It took Courtenay or his apprentice a week just to varnish all the ungilded work ("*To 7 Days Work at Varnishing . . . .£3.10—"*), and his charges totaled £81.2.11. His bill and signature receipting for payments over the next five months reveal something else: Courtenay was a fluent writer with a considerable architectural vocabulary. That didn't at all signal the end of John Cadwalader's program for sprucing up his woodwork. Thomas Nevell had paneled all three parlors for £374, and Randolph's bill of November 24, 1770, for carving in them plus two of the bedrooms came to £252.16.1. As we know by now, when the front door finally opened to the Cadwaladers' guests, they were greeted by a Winter Palace in blue and gold.

Courtenay carved other interiors for John Dickinson and in the Samuel Powel house; of all his work, apparently only fragments from the Powel house (and the two copied frames around the Cadwalader portraits) survive with attribution based on supporting documents.

There is also the curious matter of the fireplace carvings in the Blackwell house:

It happens that at least three neighboring Philadelphia houses, Cadwalader's, Samuel Powel's, and one at 224 Pine Street now called the Blackwell house, boasted the ultimate English adornment—mantelpiece carvings of scenes from mythology or Aesop's fables. John Cadwalader's *Judgment of Hercule* billed for above has been destroyed, but the others haven't. The Powel house carving pictured here is attributed to Courtenay by its present owner, the Philadelphia Museum of Art, partly because he worked in the house at the time the drawing room was being decorated. Were the Blackwell parlor panels Courtenay's work, too? Their animals, buildings, trees, and fences, compared with the Powel panel, certainly suggest so. What intrigues us still more is that these Blackwell tablets are "signed" with the same kidney-shaped

Carved tablet (detail) from the Powel house mantel shown below. This is "The Dog and the Piece of Meat," an Aesop's fable.

—Philadelphia Museum of Art

Drawing room mantelpiece in pine, from the Samuel Powel house, South Third Street, Philadelphia, built in 1765 by Charles Stedman. Hercules Courtenay is known to have carved parts of the interior.

—Philadelphia Museum of Art

Center tablet of three—fable, "The Dog and the Ox"—carved in the mantel of the Blackwell house parlor, c. 1764. The house stood at 224 Pine Street in Philadelphia. In 1936 H. F. du Pont found parts of the woodwork built into another house, and later bought more original pieces from the Philadelphia Museum of Art. He then reassembled the parlor at Winterthur.
—Courtesy, The Henry Francis du Pont Winterthur Museum

Right-hand tablet carved next to the one above. The houses, animals, trees, and fence look more than a little like those carved in the Powel house (*opposite page*), where Hercules Courtenay worked. Here is the kidney-shaped cabochon again.
—Courtesy, The Henry Francis du Pont Winterthur Museum

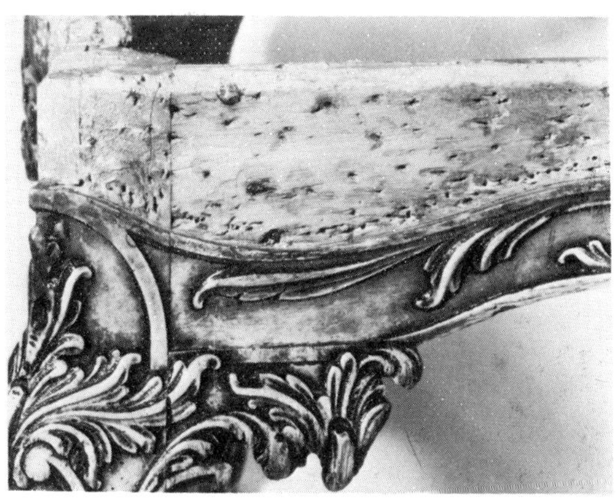

Carved cabochon in Fanshawe chair
—Courtesy of Israel Sack, Inc., N.Y.C.

cabochons found on the Fanshawe chairs. We know from the Reynolds and Courtenay gilt frames around the Cadwalader portraits that one good carver could and did make virtual duplications from another. These panels together with the chair detail point, then, if not to a single carver, to a single designer—an identity of idea, style, and technique. And it's curious that wherever this particular cabochon appears, Courtenay is never far away. Of his presumed connection with the sample chairs, S. W. Woodhouse writes: "I do not think we go too quickly in suggesting that all these chairs—as well as other similar pieces—were probably carved by Hercules Courtenay."

Considering the many similar pieces that have turned up since, I imagine Woodhouse did go too quickly. On comparing the wing chair and pair of card tables with the mantel from the Powel house, Beatrice Garvan follows Woodhouse in giving these pieces to Courtenay. However, she believes the Fanshawes as well as the scroll-foot sample chairs and marble-top pier table were carved mainly by John Pollard. Courtenay was certainly much occupied with house work.

But we have no documented carving by Pollard, nor does the evidence of his English training look solid. Randolph paid Pollard's house rent in July 1766 to a John Henderson. Other payments passed from Randolph to Pollard in the next couple of years, though he seems to fade from the record from 1768 to 1773, by which time Pollard operated as a partner with Richard Butts under the *Sign of the Chinese Shield* across from Carpenter's Hall.*

On March 24, 1767, a daughter was born to Courtenay and Mary Shute, who were wed a year later at Gloria Dei (Old Swedes') Church. The bride was then expelled from the Society of Friends for marrying *out of Meeting*, and perhaps out of season. Two more children, Daniel and Hercules Jr., were born by 1775. Meanwhile Courtenay took on an apprentice named James Connelly, decorated John Cadwalader's coach, carved some busts, and as a sideline sold candles and soap. Garvan has found in the *Pennsylvania Archives* that by 1775 he was serving as a captain in the Artillery Regiment of the militia—a little later a bombardier in his company was John Hanlin, one of Randolph's journeymen. In the confusion at the Battle of the Brandywine Courtenay abandoned his howitzer to the enemy, for which he was awarded a court-martial,

*His gravestone in St. Peter's Churchyard is lettered: "In memory of Mr. John Pollard late of this city/ Carver/ who departed this life Sept. 6, 1787 aged 47 years."

but that winter at Valley Forge Washington ordered him "pardoned without censure" (*Orderly Book of General Edward Hand*, Valley Forge, January 1778).

Like Randolph, Courtenay never went back to his trade. From 1779 he and his wife ran a tavern in Philadelphia, their dwelling being assessed for the 1783 city tax at £900. He died soon after, October 26, 1784, and was buried in the Friends' cemetery.

Many of these details we owe to the Philadelphia Museum's research. The museum catalogue adds that Hercules Courtenay's line runs to a Sir William Courtenay of Kilrush, County Westmeath, born in 1533, and that Sir William's grandsons were Hercules, the carver's grandfather, and Edward Courtenay of Powderham, born in 1631.

Having tangled in the past year or so with the Westmeath and Cadwalader genealogies, I'd sooner be horsewhipped than set off after Courtenay's, but this account of his ancestry seems to have some things wrong with it. Kilrush isn't in County Westmeath but in Clare on Ireland's west coast. Even in Clare, a man's grandson isn't likely to be 98 years his junior! This grandson, said to be the carver's great uncle, was Edward Courtenay of Powderham. Powderham Castle is in Devonshire. Here, too, the carver would need to have a grandfather about a century his senior. All these generations sired at fifty-year intervals? By 1835 one of the Courtenays was still Earl of Devon, and while stranger things have happened, this needs us to believe too that around 1760 one of the family's cadet members was bundled off to London as a carver's apprentice.

The proposition that Hercules Courtenay was an Irish immigrant was published in *Antiques* for March 1961 by Meyric R. Rogers, then curator of the Garvan Collections. Rogers's piece, "Philadelphia via Dublin: influences in rococo furniture," is a fascinating one. Its theme is that close parallels run between Dublin's furniture and decorative plasterwork on the one hand and rococo carving in Philadelphia on the other. As likely carriers of this regional treatment to America's shores Rogers names Plunket Fleeson and Hercules Courtenay:* "Emigration

*By 1742 Fleeson supplied chairs as well as upholstery, and in 1755 added a military outfitting sideline:

PLUNKET FLEESON—Made and to be sold by Plunket Fleeson. at the easy Chair, in Chestnut-Street. Several Sorts of good Chair-frames, black and red leather Chairs, finished cheaper than any made here, or imported from Boston, and in Case of any defects, the Byer shall have them made good; an Advantage not to be had in the buying of Boston from Ireland . . . continued throughout the century, and many Irish-trained craftsmen were among the immigrants. Well-known examples in Philadelphia are Plunket Fleeson, paper stainer, active after 1739, and Hercules Courtenay, carver, active before the Revolution." Rogers has taken a photo of carving applied to a rococo bookcase in the Trinity College Library, Dublin, and its foliated C-scrolls look more than a little like those on the sample wing chair. His picture really jerks our electrocardiogram! Could Courtenay have turned out both the Fanshawes *and* sample chairs in Ireland, then carried only the samples to Philadelphia?

No, Courtenay couldn't have (or we'd all better go into another line of work!), and Rogers's choice of both these candidates seems in one detail to have been misdirected.

Fleeson did begin advertising in 1739, but he was born in Philadelphia in 1712. How did Rogers get the wrong ticket here? He was led down the garden path by Fleeson himself, whose *Pennsylvania Gazette* ad of August 1, 1739, says "*lately from London and Dublin, at the Sign of the Easy Chair, near Mr. Hamilton's in Chestnut Street.*" Actually, Fleeson was *from London and Dublin* in the same way an Arab doctor in Kuwait is from the Massachusetts General Hospital—which is to say, he went over there to find out how you do it. There he *sarvfed his time.*

Our sole evidence of Hercules Courtenay's English or Irish birth is his ads worded like Fleeson's, announcing himself as "*from London.*" Then what we've got to say is that Courtenay, like Fleeson, Peale, and countless others, may have been a native American who made the voyage to the mother country so he might bring back a vocation.

Wherever he was born, Courtenay certainly did go to London before 1765, and what he got there was his skill at carving "*in the newest Taste.*" Possibly he also carried to Philadelphia some of the paper patterns from which chair designs were transferred to wood.

The Fanshawes are untypical of the Scottish-born maker Thomas Affleck, and we may as well allow the abundance of their carving to be

Chairs, besides the Damage they receive by the Sea; Good live Geese Feathers, Sea beds, bed-bottoms of good Duck at 20s, and all kinds of Upholsterers Work done after the best manner. N. B. He has a neat japan'd Chest of Drawers to be sold Cheap.

—*Pennsylvania Gazette*, September 23, 1742

PLUNKET FLEESON—Pike-Heads, Halberd-heads, Drums and Colours, for completely furnishing a Company of Foot, may be had reasonably of Plunket Fleeson, in Fourth-street.

—*Pennsylvania Gazette, August 7, 1755*

untypical of Randolph, too. In fact, no chairs like these and their sister samples have come out of Philadelphia before or since. They're an attempt to introduce the Paris salons and the drawing rooms of Corsham Court, Wiltshire, into Quaker City, and Garvan may be right in suggesting that John Cadwalader and Courtenay could have been behind the whole thing, sample chairs and all. However this may have been, Randolph had to go to London engravings just to get the baubles for his trade card, and we'd be naive to suppose he made this princely furniture without a more vital link to the high-style products of St. Martin's Lane. His link seems to have been Courtenay.

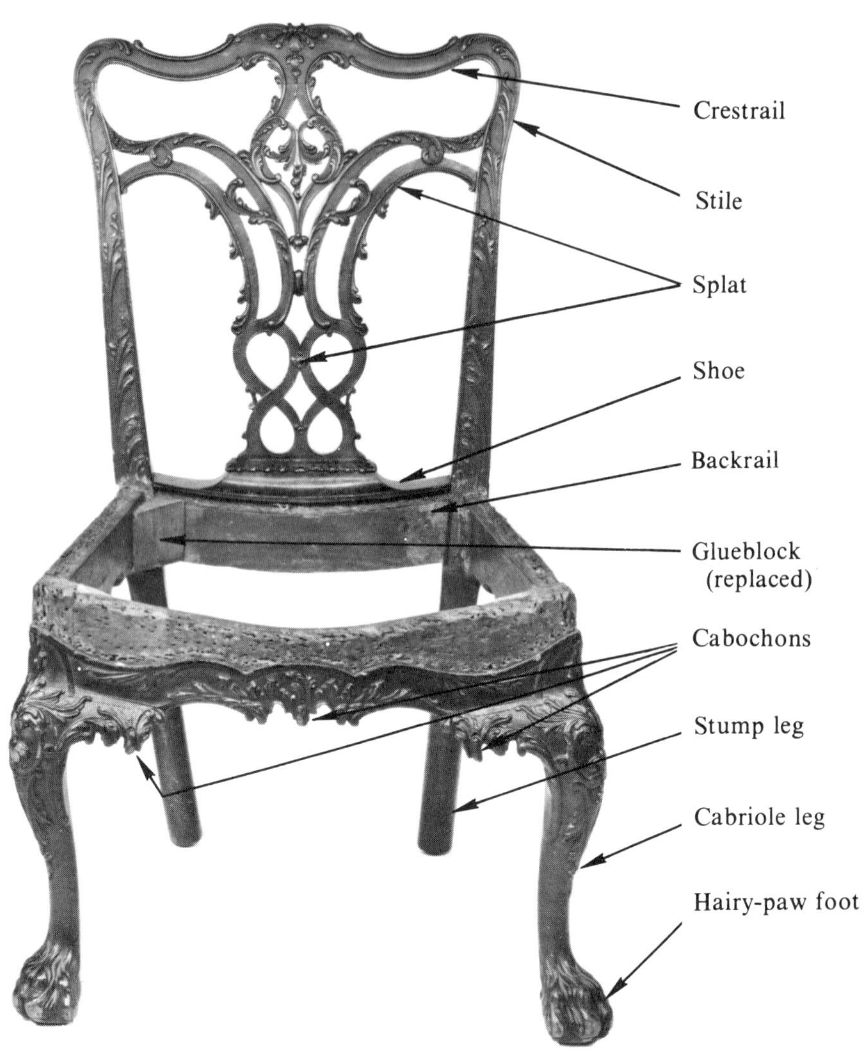
Crestrail
Stile
Splat
Shoe
Backrail
Glueblock
(replaced)
Cabochons
Stump leg
Cabriole leg
Hairy-paw foot

Appendix 4

SECOND SAMPLE AND FANSHAWE CHAIRS

Origin Philadelphia, c. 1769. Attributed to Benjamin Randolph.*
Mahogany and American eastern white cedar, 36⅞ x 21⅞ x 18⅜″ (93.7 x 55.6 x 46.7 cm)
Hairy-paw foot, acanthus-carved knee, dipped seat, leaf-carved seat frame and back.

Maker's Number	Owner (1978)	Original Corner Blocks (all others missing or replaced)	Writing on Splat Shoe
II	H. F. du Pont Winterthur Museum (Second sample chair)	1 front—white cedar 2 rear—arborvitae†	
VII	Metropolitan Museum of Art, New York	2 front—white cedar half 1 rear—?	*C. Hanlon* *John Wannamakers* *Phila*
VIII	Privately owned Philadelphia, Pa.	1 front—white cedar half 1 front—white cedar	
VIIII	Privately owned Norfolk, Va.	1 front—white cedar	*C. Hanlon* *J Wannamaker*
X	Privately owned Norfolk, Va.	2 front—white cedar	
XIII	Colonial Williamsburg	2 front—white cedar	

*The Fanshawe five are recorded by Sotheby Parke Bernet (*Art at Auction,* 1974-75) as "Chippendale carved mahogany hairy-paw foot side chairs, attributed to Benjamin Randolph, Philadelphia c. 1770. New York $207,500 (£90,217) 16.xi.74."

†Believed original at Winterthur. The only original rear block material in the Fanshawes is a fragment in chair VII; whether this also may be arborvitae is unknown. It's been suggested that carved strips or face-pieces were originally applied to the rails, edging the seat covers. In this Winterthur doesn't concur.

Thank You Note

A few of the people below have been kind enough to take the better part of a day in talking with me. Letters from others, occasionally enclosing pictures, have added only a single detail—and not usually the one I was hoping for! It's in the nature of things that not all will agree I have gotten the Fanshawe chair history exactly right. However this may prove to be, I've taken care not to fiddle in any material way with what they've said or written. Their help, so generously given, is warmly appreciated.

Walter Armytage, Moyvore, County Westmeath
Jonathan Bourne, Sotheby's, London
Captain John Cadwalader, USN, Ret., Blue Bell, Pennsylvania
David de Boinville, British Embassy, Washington, D.C.
Ronald A. De Silva, Ronald A. De Silva Inc., New York
Father P. K. Egan, Portumna, County Galway
Jonathan Fairbanks, Museum of Fine Arts, Boston, Mass.
Major R. G. Fanshawe, Stow-on-the-Wold, Gloucestershire
Alexandra R. Garfield, Dietrich Brothers Americana Corporation, Reading, Pennsylvania
Beatrice B. Garvan, Philadelphia Museum of Art, Philadelphia
Morrison H. Heckscher, Metropolitan Museum of Art, New York
David Hone, Dublin
Graham Hood, Colonial Williamsburg Foundation, Williamsburg, Virginia
Charles F. Hummel, Henry Francis du Pont Winterthur Museum, Winterthur, Delaware
Marion Day Iverson, Westgate, Maryland
Noel Judd, Battersby & Co., Dublin
Mr. and Mrs. Francis Martyn, Pallas, Tynagh, County Galway
Hugh Nugent, Ballinlough Castle, Clonmellon, County Westmeath
William A. Nugent, 13th Earl of Westmeath, Bradfield, Reading, Berks.
Archdeacon Ryan, St. Michael's Church, Tipperary, County Tipperary
Harold Sack, Israel Sack, Inc., New York
Stan Shields, *Connacht Tribune & Sentinel*, Galway, County Galway
Leo Smith, Dawson Gallery, Dublin
William Stahl, Sotheby Parke Bernet, Inc., New York
George Stapleton, E. & G. Stapleton, Dublin
John A. H. Sweeney, Henry Francis du Pont Winterthur Museum, Winterthur, Delaware

Berry B. Tracy, Metropolitan Museum of Art, New York
Nicholas B. Wainwright, Historical Society of Pennsylvania, Philadelphia
John Walsh, Flower Hill, Tynagh, County Galway

D.L.

Index

(Roman numerals show seniority but not always lineal descent.)

A

B

C

D

E

F

G

H

I

J

K

L

M

N

O

P

R

S

T

Z